The Reigning Error

The reigning error of mankind is, that we are not content with the conditions on which the goods of life are granted.

Samuel Johnson, *The Rambler*, Number 178, November 30, 1751.

The Reigning Error

The Crisis of World Inflation

WILLIAM REES-MOGG

HAMISH HAMILTON
LONDON

First published in Great Britain 1974 by Hamish Hamilton Ltd
90 Great Russell Street, London WC1

Copyright © 1974 by William Rees-Mogg

SBN 241 89155 8 cased

SBN 241 89163 9 paper

332. 414

REE

Printed in Great Britain by
Tonbridge Printers Ltd, Peach Hall Works, Tonbridge, Kent

Contents

Acknowledgements

This essay developed from an article I wrote for *The Times* on May 1, 1974, which I have republished as an appendix. I published that article almost as a freelance contribution to my own newspaper; my views on monetary policy are broadly shared by my senior economic colleagues on *The Times,* but *The Times* is not committed to gold as a newspaper.

I should, however, like to thank Peter Jay and Hugh Stephenson for the very instructive discussions we have had on economic policy; both of them read the manuscript and I am grateful for that. I should also like to thank Tim Congden for help with the nineteenth-century statistics in the original article.

I am grateful to Sir Arnold Weinstock, Nils Taube and Bernard Levin for reading the proofs and discussing them; they naturally bear no responsibility for the views expressed. In addition I am grateful to my wife, Gillian, and to my family, for letting me write the book on our August holiday, and to my secretary, Miss Elizabeth Stevens, for typing it at great speed and with great accuracy.

I should also like to thank the authors and publishers of the following books from which I have quoted. Sir Roy Harrod and Macmillan & Co. Ltd., *The Life of John Maynard Keynes;* The Royal Economic Society, Lord Keynes' letter to the *Economist,* 1933; Professor Mary Douglas, her letter to *The Times* of August 3, 1974; A. J. P. Taylor and the Clarendon Press, *English History 1914–1945;* Professor Golo Mann and Chatto & Windus, *The History of Germany since 1789* (translated by Marion Jackson); Storey, Boeckh & Associates, *The Bank Credit Analyst;* Paul Roazen and Alfred A. Knopf, Inc., *Freud: Political and Social Thought;* Professor Milton Friedman, Anna Jacobson Schwartz and Princeton University Press, *A Monetary History of the United States, 1867–1960;* Christopher Hollis and William Heinemann Ltd., *The Seven Ages;* Thomas Nelson & Sons Ltd., *An Outline Of Money* by Geoffrey Crowther.

CHAPTER ONE

PROMETHEUS UNBOUND

The ordinances of the Torah are not a burden, but a means
of ensuring mercy, kindness and peace in the world.

Maimonides (1135–1204)

Inflation is a disease of inordinacy. There are other such
diseases: the extremes of human government, anarchy and
tyranny, represent the inordinacy of the people and the inordinacy of the ruler; cancer is an inordinacy of the cellular
system in which the cells cease to obey the rules which control
their reproduction; inflation is an inordinacy of money. It is
money without order.

From the earliest times mankind has been afraid of inordinacy
and conscious of the temptation it represents to the human
mind. The Old Testament is a dialogue of inordinacy and
rebuke between the children of Israel and their God; the earliest
myths of the Old Testament, those myths which grip the
imagination even of children, the loss of Paradise, the Flood,
the Tower of Babel, are myths about the temptation of inordinacy and its consequences. The ancient Greek myths have
a similar character. Greek tragedy is concerned with the inevitable punishment of hubris, an inordinate human pride. The
myths of Icarus, who flew too near the sun, of Prometheus, who
was punished for bringing fire to earth, or of Phaeton, who
borrowed the chariot of the sun, are myths with the nature of
warnings.

The problem of inordinacy, like the problem of inflation, is
not a new one; it is rooted in the nature of man, as inflation is
rooted in the nature both of man and of money. We may live
in a century with a particular tendency to inordinacy, but we
are repeating, in the pattern of our time, one of the recurrent
dramas of history. Every generation, every movement, which
has tried to reject the limitations of humanity, has been involved

9

in the same delusion and has suffered similar and similarly inevitable consequences. Equally, in the search for ordinacy, for order, for the means of controlling human nature, we are dealing with a matter that goes back to the earliest known periods of human history.

Perhaps the most instructive experience is that of the Jewish people themselves, though one can draw parallels in the history of any other nation. To the Christian, whose God is a Jewish Messiah, the sufferings of the Jewish people show the same truth through sorrows as the suffering of Jesus Himself. In the Gemara, written in the mid-period of the Roman Empire, it is told that the Rabbis say: 'If anyone comes nowadays and desires to become a proselyte, they say to him: "Why do you want to become a proselyte? Do you not know that the Israelites are harried, hounded, persecuted and harassed, and that sufferings befall them?" If he says, "I know it, and I am not worthy," they receive him without further argument.'

The wisdom of suffering is the wisdom of humility. It is prosperity that tempts men to forget the limits of human nature and the limits of human power. Suffering educates men to accept their own limited natures in the same way that the discipline of a parent, however gentle, educates a child to accept ordinacy as an individual.

In a time of survival, we need to ask how the Jews survived, and not merely survived physically, but survived as a spiritual nation. They have no doubt survived because of the strength of the family, yet that itself is owing to the Torah and the Talmud, the Bible and the Law. The Torah is what Christians know as the Old Testament; the Talmud consists of the rabbinical books of law and commentary which were created in the early centuries after the destruction of Jerusalem in AD 70. As one commentator has written: 'The aim of the creators of the Talmud was to preserve the homeless Jews by surrounding them with a Wall of Law no matter where they might be forced to roam.'

It is this ancient tradition of law which gives such characteristic authority to rabbinical thought. A rabbi is not expressing an opinion, still less is he indulging in a sentiment. He is interpreting a law, with both the text and the accumulated precedent of previous interpretation to guide him. He has the intellectual precision of a judge, relying on an absolute standard.

This systematic lucidity is the mark of Jewish thought, obvious in orthodox Jewish thinking on religious subjects, but also present in Jewish thinking in general, so that the same characteristic of interpreting from systematic laws is to be found in Marx and Freud, and has made Marx and Freud so formidable and to some minds so fascinating. Marxism is indeed almost an inversion of the rabbinical view of the world; it is the Talmud of the devil. One of the gifts of Jewish culture to Christianity is that it has taught Christians to think like Jews, and any modern man who has not learned to think as though he were a Jew can hardly be said to have learned to think at all.

The system of rabbinical studies is to be revered for its religious quality; it is a Christian misunderstanding that Judaism as a religion became merely or drily legalistic during the Christian era. Judaism is filled with the understanding of God. But for the historian, rather than the student of theology, its interest lies in its contribution to the survival of the Jewish nation. It provided a standard by which action could be tested, a law for the regulation of conduct, a focus for loyalty and a boundary for the energy of human nature.

The Jewish people are, after all, a people of an electric energy, both of personality and of mind. Leaving aside the personality of Jesus, whom Christians do and Jews do not believe to have been the Messiah, the historic impacts of Jews on mankind have been made by men such as Moses, St Paul, Maimonides, Karl Marx, Freud and Einstein. Beside such men our own dear Disraeli is merely a *flâneur*. For one small nation to have produced such men is as though they had thrown so many atom bombs on the table of history.

Indeed, nuclear physics provides the best analogy to the way in which the integrity and purpose of the Jewish people has been preserved by the law. In the attempts which have been made to harness nuclear fusion – the power of the hydrogen bomb rather than that of the atom bomb – the problem which has so far defeated the scientists has been to control the energy of the reaction. Attempts have been made to hold the plasma of energy together, for only the briefest of periods, by wrapping it in a magnetic field from which it cannot break out. That wrapping is called a magnetic bottle.

In the same way, the energy of the Jewish people has been enclosed in a different type of container, the law. That has acted as a bottle inside which this spiritual and intellectual energy could be held; only because it could be held has it been possible to make use of it. It has not merely exploded or been dispersed; it has been harnessed as a continuous power. If energy is not contained it cannot be used over a period of time. Contained energy can be a driving force over an indefinite period; uncontrolled energy is merely a big and usually destructive bang. In human nature only disciplined energy is effective.

It is easy to think of a long list of these systems of containing energy. Some are merely human disciplines, such as the military discipline which controls the killing energy of an army, or the education which controls and channels the native energy of the individual. Others are systems which convert inanimate forms of energy, of steam or petrol, into the consistent energy which is required to drive a machine. Yet others, and these include some of the most interesting and instructive, are the laws which make games possible. If inflation is an economic system running out of control we have to find such a rule of order if we are ever to end inflation.

All these systems of control have in common one simple principle. They set limits; they establish boundaries. In the case of some of them the limits they establish are purely conventional in character. There is no reason why an over in cricket should consist of six balls rather than seven, though there is a reason why an over should not be infinitely long, or even consist of fifty balls. In other cases the limits are conventional markers to real boundaries: a white line in the centre of the road is a conventional marker which points to the real fact that the traffic on the other side of the road is flowing in the opposite direction.

The systems of law, as opposed to arbitrary power, have another characteristic in common. They set boundaries, but they do not seek to inhibit the energy that may be used inside the terms that they set. The internal combustion engine turns an explosion into a progression, but it does not simultaneously water the petrol. Just laws limit human conduct, but leave human conduct free inside those limits, even where, as in the laws concerning Jewish orthodox observances – or indeed the laws of cricket – the limits are strict. The implicit corollary of all systems of laws, political or moral, is that man is free where he is not forbidden, though it is for him to make use of his freedom. Indeed freedom is only possible inside a system of law; where no actions are excluded, no effective action is possible.

All successful systems for containing energy treat energy as though it were extremely, perhaps infinitely, great and extremely, perhaps infinitely, valuable. The first is certainly true. If there were no limits and no friction, which is a type of limit, the energy from the fall of a grain of shot would explode the universe. Yet life itself is an expression of energy : the value of energy is the value of life itself.

Just before the last war Mr Christopher Hollis, the English Roman Catholic author, was teaching in Notre-Dame, the American Roman Catholic university. He met there Waldemar Gurian, the German savant, who was both a Jew by nationality and a Roman Catholic by religion. In his memoirs Hollis writes : 'Gurian's basic position was quite simple. Hitler was the devil. His regime was as evil as could be. There had been other evil men in history. Bismarck was an evil man. He wanted things to which he was not entitled. But Bismarck was an "ordinate" man, as he called him. His ambitions were limited. He knew when to stop. If you granted what he wanted you could do business and make a bargain with him. Hitler was an "inordinate" man. There was no possibility of satisfying him, of making a bargain with him. . . . "But in the end?" I asked. "Oh, he is mad and madness is sure to end in destruction," Gurian replied, "but he will destroy all else in destroying himself." '

Sanity consists in limitation; the inordinate is always insane and always ends in destruction. Because inflation is indeed inordinate, it too has a certain insanity about it and it naturally tends to end in an explosion of destruction, a nihilist act with money. The insanity of inflation leaves a mark of insanity on society; it changes a good society into one which, so long as inflation lasts, is wholly and fraudulently unjust. All evil is a breach of order, but only some evil is a breach of order with unlimited effect; inflation is an unlimited monetary and economic evil.

The classical periods of human history have just the opposite sense of order and of sanity about them. The Athens of Pericles, the Roman Empire of Augustus – despite the introduction of Emperor-worship – or of the Antonines, the religious culture of thirteenth-century Europe, the high periods of the Chinese dynasties, the England of George II or Victoria, all present the same picture of controlled energy. The same feeling is given by the very greatest works of art, and by the minds of the artists.

Perhaps Alexander Pope brings out the contrast of energy and control more clearly than any other poet. He is perhaps not to be ranked among the very greatest of classical poets, if only because his poetry lacks the repose, the sense of peace, which one finds in Homer, Shakespeare or Goethe. Yet the use of a highly artificial verse form, the heroic couplet, provides the strongest possible contrast between the formal container and the energy of meaning contained, between the bottle and the wine.

In his lecture on Pope, Lytton Strachey quoted the line : 'Die of a rose in aromatic pain' to show the intensity of feeling that is concentrated in Pope's poetry. One can in fact open the pages at random and find lines and passages with the same intensity of feeling to them :

> Or at the ear of Eve, familiar toad,
> Half forth, half venom, spits himself abroad.

The energy compressed in Pope's lines spits itself abroad; indeed Pope's mind was a concentrator of verbal energy, so that the tight verse form of the heroic couplet contains a concentration of meaning and emotion that a looser verse form could not be made to hold.

The other obvious example of contrast between complex and artificial forms and intense concentration of meaning is Horace. *Exegi monumentum aere perennius* – I have built a monument more lasting than brass – a monument of compacted and intense meaning, and in the formal odes to Augustus, a monument to order. One of the odes of Horace conveys more meaning, and leaves more meaning in the mind, than a history by a lesser author.

The same sense of ordinate energy is present in all the great classical works of art. In some it is present to such a degree that they seem almost alien to the modern mind. One can hear tourists say: 'I do not really like the Sistine Chapel.' It is, I suspect, the massive strength of order in the mind of Michelangelo which they find disquieting. Yet the energy is proportionate to the discipline which contains it, and perhaps that energy, the lion in the cage, also makes them uneasy.

We see the same contrast between energy and control in all the great works of the human mind. It is present in Plato as well as in Kant; it is present in Shakespeare as well as in Beethoven; it is present in Einstein as well as in Sir Isaac Newton. It is the mark of Christian sanctity, implicit in the Gospels, present in the great Popes from St Gregory the Great to Pope John XXIII, in the great founding saints from Saint Augustine, through Saint Benedict to Saint Ignatius Loyola.

The creative power of the human mind depends on this principle: without energy, form is an empty tomb; without form, energy is chaos.

All constitutions are containers for human political action, and so are the arrangements by which constitutions are supported, the ideologies, the traditions, the symbols and the panoplies of state. The constitution of the United States has directed the political energies of the American people for all its history and, despite the Civil War, has provided an unexpected degree of stability. It is of course adjustable, but only by due and difficult process; important as the amendments have been, and important as the process of interpretation by the Supreme Court has been, the original constitution has in the main provided successfully for the changes in the political circumstances, political beliefs and population of the United States over two centuries.

It is not, however, only the formal legal requirements of a constitution which control human political action. The flag, the national anthem, the whole apparatus of patriotism, play their part. They provide a focus of loyalty for the psychic need of the people.

Or again one can look at kingcraft. The masters of kingcraft, Henry IV of France, Elizabeth I of England, Louis XIV, Catherine the Great, or earlier kings like Charlemagne, appear in power as the response to anarchy or the fears of anarchy. Kingcraft can be an alternative to constitution-making: it is a means of winning the wills of subjects by providing a focus for their imaginations.

Of these foci Versailles is the greatest physical example. Versailles is not at all to be seen as a self-indulgence, or as a monument to vainglory. It was built as a necessary machine for ruling France. The grandeur of Versailles was designed to confirm the grandeur of the King, of *Le Roi Soleil*. The ritual of Versailles was designed to control the energy and subordinate the wills of the French aristocracy. Every detail, from the particular salute with which each lady was greeted, to the vital question of rank which determined who was and who was not entitled to hassocks at royal weddings and funerals, provided for a graduated subordination. The monarchy of Louis XIV was absolute, but it was not inordinate; it was on the whole welcomed by subjects whose memories of disorder made them fear a weak monarch, who enjoyed the spectacle and the sense of dominant personality of their King.

In each age of man's history there has been the search for order, and each age had seen the failure of order. Man first emerges as a nomadic hunter, with his tribal loyalties and beliefs the frame of order which permitted survival. He then became a farmer, with the possibility of storing capital and the need for a social system which would permit him to reap in autumn where he had sown in spring.

In these earliest ages, and in all subsequent ages known to us, disorder was constantly breaking in. The fall of Greece, the exiles of Israel, the irruption of the Huns, the Dark Ages, the sacking of much of the coast of western Europe by the Danes, the sacking of France by England in the Hundred Years War, the religious wars of the sixteenth and seventeenth centuries, the world wars of the twentieth century, are all expressions of the breakdown of order between peoples or between nations.

A dying form of order can also be destroyed by the order that is ready to take its place. Failure of adaptation of social forces, as of philosophies, can destroy the old, and such destruction may be unavoidable to permit the new to develop. Yet in this century we may feel that we are come into an inordinate period, that neo-anarchy is the mark of much twentieth-century thought. If we now feel ourselves plagued by disorder, it comes from a long historic process whereby most of the bases of authority have been undermined.

There are numerous strands to this historical and psychological development. One can see its origins even from the time when the classical phase of English culture was still in its morning hours. It was as early as the 1720s that men of creative gifts first noticed and first resented the denatured quality of what Chaplin called Modern Times. *Gulliver's Travels* first appeared in 1726; Pope's *Dunciad* and Gay's *Beggar's Opera* in 1728. They are all satires of protest, and the deterioration of civilisation against which they protest foreshadows the common defects of life in the twentieth century.

The *Dunciad* is an attack on the glibness of the media, as they are now called. Northcliffe would have made a much better hero for the *Dunciad* than either Theobald or Cibber, though Northcliffe was not to be born for a century and a half and has now been dead for more than fifty years. There is no need to rewrite Pope to satirise the instant experts of television. Lord Northcliffe and the commentators are what the *Dunciad* is about, as much as poor Welsted, who in fact wrote an agreeable poem about apple pie.

It is perhaps dangerous to refer to the decline of these aspects of civilisation; after all, one cannot try to make a politic of antiquarianism. 'Where's Troy, and where's the maypole in the Strand?' The politics of Sir Robert Walpole were not edifying when they happened; it would be ridiculous to try to bring him back. Yet we shall not understand our distresses unless we are willing to recognise what we have lost. In the classic periods of history, from Socrates to Mr Asquith, the formation of opinion, both in the city and in the village, was dominated by the quiet and precise conversation of informed and serious men. In this century it has increasingly been dominated by the power of dissemination of noisy and ignorant men. We have lost much of our belief in the power of rational discussion to reach the truth, and rational discussion has consequently lost much of its power to influence the public. We are culturally under-privileged relative to our grandparents, because our means of communication are less well adapted to the identification of precise statements of truth than were theirs. At the same time, and this is welcome, such culture as we have is more widely distributed;

yet our culture is particularly vulnerable to false simplification and to the elevation of short-term gratification against longer-term interests.

If we experience this cultural deterioration, we also see the alienation of the arts of painting, sculpture and music. Here, with alarming speed, there is a march of inordinacy, a direct route march at light infantry speed. In painting the image is first simplified, then distorted, then broken, then mocked and finally discarded, only to be brought back as a final gesture of alienation and contempt. The same process is followed with the forms of music. These movements of the arts, matched by the even more terrible brutalised simplicities of totalitarian art, reflect the despair of twentieth-century culture.

All these movements have their origins in cultural history. After all, the romantic movement, the cult of energy as opposed to control, is now two hundred years old. That monstrous political romantic, Bonaparte, Byron, Shelley, the Marquis de Sade, were all dead before our grandfathers were born. Not to be a contemporary of Byron is one of the sweets of twentieth-century life. The aesthetic of romanticism matches the personalities of romanticism; it is an aesthetic of attack on order, just as Bonapartism, like Hitlerism, expresses the attempted apotheosis of personal inordinacy in politics.

We have been stripped of much of the defence of a civilisation of individual reason, and exposed to an aesthetic hostile to order; it is no wonder that we live in an inordinate period. Yet perhaps even more powerful than these cultural and aesthetic influences is the development of science. Science seems to have destroyed the limits of human life. The unfortunate Icarus fell into the sea, the Tower of Babel caused acute confusion, but today Icarus is triumphant, now that we have seen those brave and straightforward Americans walking on the surface of the moon. Man has expressed an ultimate form of hubris, and nothing appears to have happened to rebuke him for it.

Of course it is in one way absurd to associate science with inordinacy. Indeed science is concerned with finding co-ordinates, with establishing the laws of nature. Yet to the ordinary man the power of science seems to enable scientists to break those laws. The ordinary man is conscious of the ability of a supersonic airliner to reach New York in three hours. For a few days he regards that as remarkable but then he forgets about it. He is, however, left with an impression that the limits of nature have been overcome. So, as previously conceived, they have been.

What he is not conscious of is the adaptation to the limits of nature that makes this feat possible. Exactly the right shape, flying at the right angle, with the right power can alone achieve it. An airliner flies inside limits of climb and speed and stall, as though there were a moving envelope of co-ordinates around it in flight. Yet this mastery of co-ordinates creates the inordinate; it results in the increase in the power of man over his environment, which has already gone half way towards destroying the environment, and for that matter half way to destroying man. A scientific age acquires a confidence in the power of the human mind which in other regions of human activity is not justified, and is indeed not justified in the use, as opposed to the development, of scientific knowledge.

The changes of modern society in the democracies have largely been in the direction of a reduction in social structures; this has been caused by powerful economic forces, which have destroyed or greatly weakened the hierarchic individualism characteristic of nineteenth-century Europe, and to a lesser extent of the United States in the same period. A loose mixture of liberal, egalitarian and Marxist theory has furthered the change in economic organisation, and this has created new societies much less defined in structure than the old, but much larger in scale.

The distinguished anthropologist, Professor Mary Douglas, discussed the implications of this weakly structured social system in a letter to *The Times* (August 3rd, 1974) on the Annan Report on the student troubles at Essex University: 'Dr Sloman, the Vice-Chancellor, was himself in his Reith lectures in the 1960s a distinguished exponent of that view of society which is still fashionable in educational circles and still gathering force in other quarters. It supposes that people can best work together when hampered by the minimum of institutional rules, not separated by formal distinctions, but only inspired by their commitment to a common aim.

'Such a theory might do well for disembodied spirits. But

humans need their identity made visible and their responsibilities defined. Boundaries and rules enable identities to be established. When they are ambiguous, those caught in ill-defined institutions invariably resort to blame-pinning among themselves. I have argued this at length with many tribal and modern examples in *Purity and Danger* and *Natural Symbols*.

'The Annan Report is the case history of the failure of a social theory. It records the new students' sense of homelessness in the broad-based first-year course common to them all; it notes the deliberately weak spatial symbolism (no junior common room, no senior common room, no territorial identity for the teaching departments), and it notes the ambiguous allocation of responsibility. Not the Vice-Chancellor's lack of political skills but the institution's lack of structure is to blame for the place deserted at weekends, the lack of student societies, the difficulty of making friends except at student demos, the inaccessibility of staff and their low regard for simple teaching.

'In such unstructured societies we invariably find forms of witchhunting or the tendency to attribute personal blame and accept no responsibility, which Lord Annan notes. . . .'

The strong structure of liberal society in the nineteenth century was built on the independent authority of the individual, and particularly of the individual proprietor, whether in business, property ownership or the professions. Private property needs a liberal society for its security, and the values of freedom have normally rested on the economic basis of private ownership. The twentieth century has seen these individual proprietorships merged into businesses of much larger size; state-owned industry, the large international corporation, the nation-wide trade union dominate the economy and therefore dominate society. The assumptions of large-scale bureaucratic organisations permeate every aspect of national life, so that, for instance, many university students see themselves as trade unionists and the university as an employer, an analogy that would have seemed grotesque to earlier generations of students.

The mammoth business organisation, like the mammoth high-rise apartment block, has a scale out of all human proportion. It also has, or almost always has, a position of monopoly power. Monopoly naturally tends to the inordinate, because the processes of competition are themselves restrictions on the extension of power.

In communications, structure, economic system, worship of scientism, fashionable ideology, the modern world tends to the inordinate. We have eaten of the tree of knowledge and the fruit of the tree was Hiroshima. The same inordinacy is to be seen as a consequence of the decline of religion, and of the alteration of moral standards.

All religions involve a spiritual order for believers. Any man who believes in God believes in a spiritual authority other than himself, and infinitely more important than himself. His spiritual universe is one in which he is a very small and remote moon reflecting the light of an infinitely great sun, cherished and warmed by the sun, but smaller than any grain of sand beside it.

So long as he adheres to this belief, the Christian, or the Jew, Hindu, Moslem, Buddhist, or the faithful of any religion, has a sanity imposed upon him. He cannot see himself as inordinately important. He cannot be taken over by what Jung so aptly termed psychic inflation.

As religion has declined this has been an age in which men proclaimed themselves gods. How many gods we have seen : Benito Mussolini, Adolf Hitler, Joseph Stalin, Charles Manson, Idi Amin, and the eastern gods, gods of all races. One thing they all have in common. They are all killers and they are all mad, all filled with the mythical sense of their own godhood, of their own supreme importance. 'Heil Hitler . . . Sieg Heil . . . Viva il Duce . . . our beloved leader . . . our party and our Soviet Government with mighty Stalinist blows crushed and destroyed these despicable vipers, these hired agents of fascism . . . loud and prolonged applause. All rise. The hall resounds with shouts of : Long live the Great Stalin ! Hurrah for Comrade Stalin !'

It is all madness. And one can see the logic of this madness. There is no god; therefore there is no personality with authority over my personality; therefore my personality is unlimited; but there are people who oppose my will; therefore they are wicked – 'this foul riffraff, this rabid gang of spies, bandits and wreckers,' as Beria called them; therefore they must be destroyed, liquidated, there must be a final solution; only those who appreciate my superordinate quality are fit to live in our new world of Nazism/Fascism/Soviet Communism. Everyone else is a traitor. This is the logic of megalomania, most dangerous when it is pushed to the level of self-apotheosis.

This too is found in history. The Roman emperors went mad by the dozen; Alexander was mad; Napoleon Bonaparte, far more than Lord Byron himself, was mad, bad and dangerous to know. But to this grand folly, which is itself so conspicuous in our own century, there is the counterpart, a lesser, commoner madness, which affects millions. That is the madness not of the human god, but of the worshipper at the shrine of humanity, the error not of the man who believes himself omnipotent, but of him who sees no limits to the collective capacity of mankind. That is compatible with a good conscience and being a good democrat, but it is an equally serious error.

It is one of the apparently puzzling observations of Jung that religion is 'psychologically true'. There was at one time much confusion about whether by that he meant that religion was false but good for you, or whether he meant that religion was indeed true. In fact he was himself a religious man, and the point he was making was that religion was necessary to the sane development of the mind, because it corresponded to the real structure of the mind.

By contrast, Freud was not a religious man, he was reacting against the oppressive restrictions of the sexual mores of late nineteenth-century Vienna, and against the strictness of orthodox Judaism. He was looking for a liberation both for his patients and for himself.

No doubt that liberation was needed: many people were – as many are – crippled by those sexual obsessions which resulted from the unhealthy and exaggerated control of Victorian sexuality. At the same time the Freudian revolution has had ultimate social consequences probably far more damaging than the hysterias and repressions he set out to cure.

Almost equally with Marxism, the Freudian revolution was widespread, and still is. Freud's doctrines, often in a confused form, have become part of the language of modern people; we can all talk of the subconscious and of repressions. His ideas were carried by popularisers and by sympathisers – such as Dr Spock – into the field of education and the upbringing of children; they changed the world's view of education, of marriage and of sexual conduct.

In this process the original doctrines were distorted almost out of recognition, though not quite. Freud was a revolutionary and he did wish to break down the barriers of sexual morality. Yet his views have now emerged in common culture as a series of simple propositions : sex is the most important thing in life; it is unhealthy not to enjoy sex; everyone has a right to a happy sex life; all forms of sex are equally valid; there is no such thing as pornography; it is wrong to repress any sexual desires; the road to sexual and mental health is to have sexual relations early and often; any limitation on anyone else's sex life is an intolerable interference with his freedom, except when it is necessary to protect a child. Children should be left free to develop as they will.

These views in this simple form were not Freud's, but it is hard to deny that they have flowed historically from what he did think, which was itself based on the damage that sexual repression and repressed memories of a sexual kind had done to patients who went to him for help. The new licence is not what mankind has normally believed, in either advanced or primitive cultures.

Anthropological research shows that sex customs vary extremely widely, but that in all societies, or almost all societies, social objectives, the maintenance of the family, the maintenance of the economic system, the maintenance of the tribe, have been regarded as more important than freedom of sexual conduct.

This Freud himself would have accepted. He regarded the processes of civilisation as requiring a limitation both of the sexual and of the aggressive urges. The trouble is that he was ambivalent about the sexual urge, normally taking a liberationist view, partly because of his preoccupation with sick people and with their maladjustments. He also tried to distinguish between the control of sex, about which he was uncertain, and the control of aggression, about which he was much more definite, although both drives have the same source of energy. In fact the widespread decline in sexual control has been accompanied by a corresponding increase in aggression in most countries. Rape, combining sex with aggression, is becoming a much more common crime.

This problem is well discussed in Mr Paul Roazen's work *Freud: political and social thought*. He argues that psychoanalysis has developed greater understanding since Freud's death. 'It is often seen that Freud is ambivalent towards cultural restrictions, because the coercion which often stunts men's personalities is nevertheless the instrument which has made civilisation possible in the first place. But it has not been noticed that implicitly within Freud's work, and quite explicitly in psychoanalytic theory since his death, limitations are shown to have a positive directive aspect. Freud is always more articulate about the usefulness of restrictions when he is talking of the aggressive drives.'

Unfortunately, in an age when the cultural restrictions were under general attack, it was Freud's simpler message which was taken and parodied. It emerged in the form 'anything goes'.

Economists, no less than psychologists, are the children of their own age. We should therefore expect that an age which was moving towards the destruction of the old forms of order and existing authority, would find economists to lead it in the direction it wanted to go. Almost as revolutionary as the work of Freud were the doctrines developed by the great economist of the period, Maynard Keynes.

Both Freud and Keynes were men of genius. Both developed systems of genuine insight and high intellectual quality. Neither was simplistic; Keynes even more than Freud understood the multi-faceted character of truth. Yet each was reacting against the constraints of his time, and posterity has taken from the work of each what might be term its libertine quality, the quality of simplifying the short term by removing the immediate obstacles to gratification.

One can see from the work of Lytton Strachey, a close Cambridge and Bloomsbury friend of Keynes, how naturally in their time and situation hostility to established authority and established standards developed. It was the intellectual revolt of young men not merely of brilliance, but of great intellect. Strachey's *Eminent Victorians,* a book of intense feeling, is an almost Oedipal attack on the father figures of the culture of the immediate past. These men – Arnold, Manning, Gordon – were the guardians or heroes of the culture of his childhood. The young men at Cambridge mocked the gods of their fathers, as each generation tends to do, but these young men were at least the intellectual equals of the Victorian gods they mocked.

One could take one passage from Sir Roy Harrod's *Life of Keynes* and represent Keynes as attacking the previously accepted principles of political economy in the same spirit as Lytton Strachey attacked great Victorians. 'Affection for the gold standard may yet revive. Yet if it does not, the historian will record that Keynes, almost single-handed, killed that most ancient and venerable institution. It was a notable achievement, because the gold standard was perhaps the most respected and sacrosanct of all the mechanisms of nineteenth-century capitalism.'

Yet Keynes would not have put his attitude to gold in that way. In a letter of the *Economist* of March 20th, 1933, which Roy Harrod quotes, Keynes defined his attitude to gold: 'I do not know that what you call "the evolution of my ideas" is particularly important. But for the sake of accuracy I should like, in thanking you for your leading article of March 18th, to remind you that my recent advocacy of gold as an international standard is nothing new.

'At all stages of the post-war developments the concrete proposals which I have brought forward from time to time have been based on the use of gold as an international standard, whilst discarding it as a rigid national standard. The qualifications which I have added to this have been always the same, though the precise details have varied; namely, (1) that the parities between national standards and gold should not be rigid, (2) that there should be a wider margin than in the past between the gold points, and (3) that if possible some international control should be formed with a view to regulating the commodity value of gold within certain limits.

'You will find that this was my opinion in 1923 when I published my *Tract on Monetary Reform* and again in 1930 when I published my *Treatise on Money*, just as it is today, as set forth in my articles in *The Times* and in my pamphlet *The Means of Prosperity*.'

This position is entirely consistent with Keynes' line at the Bretton Woods Conference of 1944, which founded the International Monetary Fund and established the post-war gold and convertible currencies system.

We have now broken away not only from the use of gold as a national standard, but also from Keynes' own principle, the use of gold as an international standard. The people who have done so have in general thought they were acting in accordance with Keynesian principles, whilst in fact operating in opposition to Keynes' own doctrine and to his negotiating position at Bretton Woods, though at Bretton Woods he did contemplate the creation of an international paper reserve currency.

Yet the question is whether the fundamental Keynesian innovation – the dissociation between an international gold standard and a national full employment standard – was ever sound. It seemed to work from 1945 to the early 1960s, under the conditions of dollar domination of the world's currency system. Was it not inevitable that sooner or later one or other principle – the international gold standard or the national full employment standard – should prevail? What did prevail was the national full employment standard, from the early 1960s onwards, and finally in 1971. Yet the destruction of the international gold standard destroyed the basis of price stability on which the national full employment standard was designed to operate.

The essence of Keynesianism as a practical doctrine lies in this contrast. To the domestic government Keynes says that the central aim of policy is to maintain full employment through preserving a balance between demand and resources; that balance can be adjusted by deficit finance until the full employment level is reached. Until that point is reached the exchange value of the currency should be subordinated to the full employment objective. At the same time, Keynes says to the international monetary authorities that world prices should be kept stable by reference to an international gold standard.

In the special circumstances of world slump, multiple deficit finance by individual nations may be compatible with international price stability. In stable or inflationary world trading conditions they hardly can be. The contradiction was obscured in the period after the war by the fact that the United States was the predominant economy, the predominant trading partner and the predominant gold holder. The world ran not on a gold but on a dollar standard, to which other nations adjusted. The dollar standard was itself reasonably stable because the American unions were relatively weak, and the United States was therefore able to maintain stable domestic prices in the post-war period, and because the dollar was fully convertible into gold.

The psychology of Bloomsbury, of an intellectual and sexual new wave, did have an influence on Keynes, but that influence was subordinate to his great natural power as an economic theoretician. Keynes had a learned admiration for the intellectual tradition of the British school of economists, as his writings show. He regarded himself as fulfilling rather than destroying the work of Ricardo, and of Marshall who had indeed taught him at Cambridge. His writings are based on the revision of classical theory, not on its destruction. So high were his intellectual gifts that one can see the strength of the completed classical theory more clearly in his writings than perhaps in any others, except those of Marshall himself.

Keynes also had to face the problems of deflation, because it was the dominant problem of the most mature period of his work. He had the Churchillian quality of believing that one should never give in, should never accept that a problem is insoluble. Had he been facing the problems of inflation he would not be approaching them with the depressed inadequacy of the present neo-Keynesians. He would be making an attack on the theoretical foundations of this inflation.

Yet it is true that Keynesianism, like Singapore in 1941, is a fortress with all its guns pointing out to sea, and none covering the approach of a land force. It is an economic theory conceived in the light of world deflation, and it has no proper answers to world inflation. If Keynes were alive, the theory might have been extended and strengthened, but that work has not been carried out by his successors. As a result, Keynesianism today – in practice, as an influence on policy – is inflationary in effect, and consistently inflationary. When one says consistently, that means the Keynesian response over the period of any cycle will have a net inflationary effect, even though at some point in the cycle the effect may be deflationary.

If one sees the twentieth century as a historic period in which there is a great burst of inordinacy affecting the character of communications, the national and family structure, the economy of the world, men's view of religion and science, the thought of philosophers and economists, how then can one hope to stop the inordinacy of world inflation? Is not any opposition to these combined forces doomed to failure?

As a matter of months or even years, it may be so. Yet some at least of the forces or inordinacy seem to be burning themselves out. Certainly the worship of science, the false belief that science can create unlimited and benign progress, has gone into an overdue retreat. The world-wide ecological movement, resisting the inordinate exploitation of the environment, shows the spontaneous gathering of people who believe in restraint.

Though the influence of the Christian churches is probably still in decline, the willingness to accept the fact of God seems to be spreading; the certainties of agnosticism have never seemed more dubious. Man always needs the classical virtues of objectivity, of humility and of faith in the absolute and external. The hubristic pattern is always one of ambition which soars to a climax and, falling, is quenched in catastrophe. We are now on the edge of catastrophe; that means we may also be on the edge of a return to sanity.

CHAPTER TWO

THE ASSIZE OF MONEY

Evil consequences might ensue from a sudden and great reduction of the circulation as well as from a great addition to it.

David Ricardo (1772–1823)

The circumstances which predispose a society to inflation are of a varied and complex kind. There is therefore room for many views about the ultimate causes of inflation, and these views may all have some truth in them. They remain very confusing to the public, which feels that inflation is an abstract subject on which the economists themselves disagree. There is still more disagreement among politicians, some of whom have no proper understanding of the subject, all of whom are subject to political pressures, often to do the wrong thing.

I am convinced, have become convinced, that there is a single mechanism of inflation, which can be isolated and described. I do not take the view that this mechanism, which is a monetary one, operates in a vacuum. It is subject to external, non-monetary influences in its inception and at every stage of its progression. Nevertheless, there is one difference between the mechanism and the influences from outside. The mechanism is always the same. A monetary account of any inflation always shows the same pattern of operation. The outside factors are often quite different.

One can see this both historically and geographically. In the French inflation of the 1790s the prime non-monetary force was the French Revolution and the hazards that it faced; in the German inflation of 1921 to 1923 the prime non-monetary force was the reparations question and the French occupation of the Ruhr; in the German inflation after 1945 the prime non-monetary force was defeat; in the current British inflation it is trade union power. In all these inflations the basic monetary pattern has been the same.

Currently one can make the same point geographically; Japan, Italy, France, Britain and the United States are all suffering severe inflation. The non-monetary factors, mainly trade union power and oil price movements (in so far as those are regarded as political and monopolistic) differ very much from country to country. The temptation to blame oil prices is probably at its highest in Japan.

This distinction between an unchanging mechanism of inflation and changing political forces seems to me to be crucial. If one can master the mechanism then one can master inflation; yet if the mechanism is brought into operation by political forces, one will only be allowed to master the mechanism if one can also master or bring under persuasion the political forces.

If this view is correct it follows first of all that any non-monetary approach will fail. For instance, the recent Conservative attempt in Britain to combine inflationary monetary policies with control of inflation by non-monetary means was bound to be self-defeating. Yet at the same time the simplistic monetary view that it is possible by monetary means alone to control inflation is erroneous. Governments inflate because they feel that they have no political alternative but to inflate. They may or may not understand the dangers of inflating, but they act as they do in response to political forces. Those forces cannot simply be disregarded. Apart from anything else, in a democracy those forces may express themselves in an election victory for another party.

My views of the causes of inflation are not original; they belong indeed to the broad tradition of monetary economics. Nevertheless they represent a view of the character of inflation which is not universally accepted.

I find in conversation that this view of inflation is continuously interrupted by 'yes, but . . .'. Although it is traditional, it is in some way unfamiliar, and there is a natural tendency to doubt and question it. There is also a difficulty in explaining the mechanism, as I believe it to be, in one sustained piece of argument and analysis. In some ways it is as difficult as it would be to write an account of how a clock works which would provide someone who was not a clockmaker with a useful understanding of that machinery.

There is also the need to make room for objections, at least for the natural objections which anyone might be expected to take on hearing this account for the first time. I have therefore cast the argument as though it had to be presented to court. It is no bad thing to imagine oneself having to argue a case before a tough-minded judge. In order to stimulate my imagination I chose Jeffreys, who 'conducted the bloody assize after Monmouth's rebellion, as the judge to preside over the court. He was in fact a much worse man than I have portrayed him.

'Do you promise to tell the truth, the whole truth and nothing but the truth, so help you God?'

'I do.'

JEFFREYS. Prisoner at the bar, you come here charged with a most heinous and abominable offence, that is, pretending by various spells and necromancies to foretell the future, contrary to the interest and credit of Her Majesty's liege subjects. You are further charged with posing as an economist. How plead you, guilty or not guilty?

PRISONER. Not guilty, m'lud.

JEFFREYS (aside). I never saw a more villainous rogue in all my life. I'll swear if he is an economist, I'll get it out of him. Prisoner, you write about this word 'inflation'. Pray tell the court, what do you mean by this word 'inflation'?

PRISONER. By inflation I mean bad money, that is money which does not hold its value.

JEFFREYS. If money does not hold its value, what happens then?

PRISONER. Prices rise.

JEFFREYS. Then inflation is simply rising prices.

PRISONER. No, m'lud. Prices can rise for reasons which have nothing to do with inflation. A sudden rise in demand, an unexpected shortage of supply will cause prices to rise. The price of wheat rises after a bad harvest; that is the price mechanism doing its job. If the price of wheat rises after a good harvest, that is probably inflation.

JEFFREYS. Then how do you tell which are your normal healthy price increases and which your inflation?

PRISONER. Over time, ordinary price increases are balanced by price reductions. A bad harvest pushes prices up, a good one causes them to fall. Greater demand for copper pushes up the copper price, a new mine is opened and they fall. That is the normal operation of the system. With inflation there is a general tendency for prices to rise, and correspondingly for money to purchase less.

JEFFREYS. Is not this inflation some new and devilish invention of the economists, for which they thoroughly deserve to be whipped at the cart's tail through the City of London? There was no inflation in my father's day.

PRISONER. By no means, m'lud. Inflation is as old as money. It often takes people by surprise, but it is as frequently recurring as any of the plagues which affect mankind.

JEFFREYS. Tell me of these inflations. I did not read of them in my school books.

PRISONER. There were famous inflations in classical times; Alexander the Great was troubled by inflation, or at least his people were; the Roman Empire was given to inflations, and many say was finally destroyed by them.

JEFFREYS. I see you make out a respectable classical ancestry for this modern bastardy. What then caused the inflations?

PRISONER. The same thing as causes all inflations, too much money.

JEFFREYS. Explain yourself. I do not see how one can have too much money.

PRISONER. Money is only good for buying things. If there is an increase in the supply of money, but no increase in the supply of things, then money will buy less.

JEFFREYS. How came this to happen with Alexander?

PRISONER. When he invaded Asia he conquered the capitals of powerful princes, and with them the gold hoards they had accumulated. That gold increased his money supply with no corresponding increase in productive capacity. There was an increase in money not balanced by an increase in things.

JEFFREYS. And the Caesars, did they also conquer great stores of gold?

PRISONER. The Caesars had soldiers to pay and were short of money with which to pay them, so they clipped the coinage and reduced its quality to make the gold and silver go further.

JEFFREYS. Then the great Caesars defrauded their soldiers, like a common innkeeper passing a bad shilling.

PRISONER. Indeed m'lud, they did so, and all inflations, except for those which have begun in an increase in the gold supply, have fraud at the heart of them.

JEFFREYS. You speak of the gold inflations; which are those?

PRISONER. Alexander's is the first. The Spanish discovery of the gold in the New World is the second. The opening of the South African gold field is the third. In each case the increase was in good money, in gold of fine quality, but the rapid increase in the money supply in each case caused inflation, caused higher prices.

JEFFREYS. You say too much gold can do it, and adulterating the coinage can do it. I have hanged many a counterfeiter; perhaps it would have been as well to hang the Caesars. I do not see how inflation can result both from making the currency better and from making it worse.

PRISONER. M'lud, it is a question of quantity. If the effect is to increase the supply of money, it does not matter initially if that increase is in gold or in light weight. The effect is that the supply of money increases faster than the supply of goods.

JEFFREYS. Do all inflations come from too much gold or from debasing the coinage?

PRISONER. No, m'lud. The inflations of the eighteenth century came mostly from the issue of paper money. France had two such inflations, Law's inflation of 1720, and the assignat inflation of the 1790s.

JEFFREYS. We have, then, inflations from too much gold, from the state reducing the value of its own money, and from paper money. Is that all?

PRISONER. No, m'lud, we have had in the twentieth century inflations which were the result of an increase in the money supply through credit.

JEFFREYS (taking up his quill pen, writes: 'twentieth century: credit') This is too hard for me; I tell you, since I was appointed the vacation Judge in Purgatory, your twentieth century has been the most bloody and confusing age I have seen. Who creates this credit?

PRISONER. Governments do. They spend more than they raise in taxation, and they make up the difference by creating more money. This money then circulates through the banking system. It is not new gold, or clipped coin, or paper notes, but it is the creation of money nonetheless.

JEFFREYS. Prisoner, I want you to consider very carefully before you answer this question. Is there any inflation that you have ever heard of, or studied, that did not originate in an increase in the supply of money, by one of these means, that is by more gold, by debasement, by paper or by credit, which is after all paper in a different form? Remember that you are on oath.

PRISONER. No, not one. I do not believe that there is one, or could possibly be one, unless there were a destruction of the ability to supply goods.

JEFFREYS. Can you produce any authorities?

PRISONER. Perhaps I could first introduce the work *An Outline of Money* by Geoffrey Crowther, an eminent man who was Editor of the *Economist*. The relevant quotation is to be found on page 123. 'The correlation between changes in gold-mining and long-term changes in prices in the nineteenth century is far too close to be dismissed as a coincidence. We can safely say that the changes in the quantity of money in existence (or, more accurately, changes in the rate of increase in the quantity of money relative to the rate of increase in the volume of business) *caused* the changes in the value of money.' Lord Crowther was not simply a monetarist; he believed, for instance, that restriction of the money supply would prevent prices rising, but that the converse did not hold, that an increase in money supply during a depression would not necessarily cause prices to rise. If people increased their cash holdings, an increase in the money supply might be inoperative.

JEFFREYS. Nevertheless he considered that changes in the money supply do *cause* changes in value?

PRISONER. Yes, m'lud.

JEFFREYS. Have you other authorities?

PRISONER. I should be hard put to it to find authorities in the contrary sense. I do not know of an economist who would assert that he had identified an inflation which did not start with an increase in the money supply. Perhaps, however, I could introduce into evidence the view of Professor Milton Friedman. He is a monetarist; he goes beyond Crowther in relating economic changes to monetary changes. One of his major works, in collaboration with Professor Anna Jacobson Schwartz, is *A Monetary History of the United States, 1867–1960*. It is a most fascinating work.

JEFFREYS. It does not exactly sound like bedside reading.

PRISONER. I assure you, m'lud, I have it by my bedside every night.

JEFFREYS. What were Professor Friedman's findings?

PRISONER. The authors of this work state : 'Throughout the near-century examined in detail we have found that : (1) Changes in the behaviour of the money stock have been closely associated with changes in economic activity, money income and prices; (2) The interrelation between monetary and economic change has been highly stable; (3) Monetary changes have often had an independent origin; they have not been simply a reflection of changes in economic activity'.

JEFFREYS. If the Court accepts that, then it follows that the Court must accept the view that inflation originates in an increase in the supply of money. In that case the question of inflation is surely a very simple matter. Stabilise the supply of money and you stop the inflation.

PRISONER. That is what Mr Enoch Powell says, m'lud.

JEFFREYS. But do you not agree with him?'

PRISONER. I do not wholly agree with him. I think he is right to emphasise the supply of money as the cause of inflation. I do not think he gives adequate attention to the prior question.

JEFFREYS. To what prior question?

PRISONER. To the question of why the supply of money was increased in the first place.

JEFFREYS. That surely must be different from case to case.

PRISONER. Yes indeed it is, m'lud. Historically much the most common cause has been war. In war, production for ordinary needs falls; it may be disrupted by the war itself, it may be turned over to military use and needs; at the same time money has to be spent, on the purchase of equipment, on the pay of the soldiers. War is therefore by its nature inflationary; it reduces the supply of goods and puts pressure on governments to increase the supply of money.

JEFFREYS. But we are not at war now, and the rate of inflation is higher than when we were.

PRISONER. I am not saying that the present, or every inflation

35

is caused by war; plainly it is not. I give war as the strongest instance of a general truth, that the men who are actually inflating the money supply do not believe themselves to be initiating a process, but to be responding in the only possible way to the pressure of events. That is why one has to try to understand the reasons which lead to the expansion of the money supply, even if one is totally convinced of the direct link between the expansion of the money supply and inflation.

JEFFREYS. Perhaps you could give instances of that.

PRISONER. M'lud, I would like to take the great German inflation of 1921–23, the classic example of a modern total inflation, in which the purchasing power of money fell to zero.

JEFFREYS. I remember that inflation, it was a breeding ground for the Nazis.

PRISONER. Quite so, m'lud. This was a very extreme inflation; by November 1923 a loaf of bread cost 428 million marks. Now one can easily show that this inflation followed an entirely characteristic monetary pattern. During the war there had been an increase of 340 per cent in the German money supply; this had been matched by an increase of only 139 per cent in the price level. This again is not unusual; in wartime, for patriotic and other reasons, people do build up their savings. More surprisingly, the first months after the war showed a further increase in the money supply of 57 per cent between November 1918 and July 1919. Prices rose fast, but still not quite so fast as the money supply. Then, between August 1919 and February 1920, there was a period in which prices caught up, an 185 per cent rise in prices, only a 33 per cent increase in the money supply. After another pause there was a further period in May 1921 to July 1922, when money supply rose by 149 per cent, but prices rose by 635 per cent.

JEFFREYS. Prisoner, are you not destroying your own case? Here we have the early stages of the German inflation, the early stages, mark you, and prices rise four times as fast as the supply of money. If the money supply controlled the price level, that could not happen.

PRISONER. M'lud, you have put your finger on a most delicate point. It does not break the link between inflation and the money supply, but it does invalidate the quantity theory of money in its simplest form.

JEFFREYS. Prisoner, you have to explain the discrepancy. First you argue that there is a close relationship between the behaviour of the money supply and the behaviour of prices, and then you show me prices in Germany going up more than four times as fast as the stock of money.

PRISONER. M'lud, there are three explanations; all these have to be taken into account. First there is a time lag, of varying duration, between changes in the money supply and changes in prices. In Germany the wartime increase in the money supply had not been used up, and was still available to finance higher prices in 1921.

JEFFREYS. Is there any regularity in this time lag?

PRISONER. Very little. Professor Friedman shows that it can vary from the almost instantaneous to a period of a few years. Its length seems to be determined by expectation; if a movement in the money supply is working against what people expect it may take a long time to work its way through; if it reinforces expectation, it may be almost instantaneous.

JEFFREYS. Let me make sure I am getting this right. Your argument is that an inflation invariably starts with an increase in the money supply, though that increase may itself be due to a political event, such as war. Is that right so far?'

PRISONER. Yes, m'lud.

JEFFREYS. Then the timing of the impact of an increase in the money supply will be affected by a time lag, which may be longer or shorter according to expectations the public have about their economic prospects. Is that right?

PRISONER. Absolutely right, m'lud.

JEFFREYS. Well, so far you have not, I think, gone outside the comprehension of the average jury. You will do so at your peril. What else decides the effects of an increase in the money supply?

PRISONER. Velocity, m'lud.

JEFFREYS. Here I think you are about to escape me, and my constant ruling is that what I do not understand cannot be good law.

PRISONER. M'lud, people do not like to think about velocity.

JEFFREYS. I am not at all sure that I like to think about velocity. What does it mean?

PRISONER. It expresses the rate at which money circulates. We talk about the stock of money, or the money supply, but the availability of money depends not only on quantity but on circulation. The faster the circulation the more business a given quantity of money can transact. It is like the art of war, which depends not only on how many troops the general has but also the speed with which he can move them to the crucial point.

JEFFREYS. What you are saying is that it makes no difference whether you have twice the quantity of money or twice the velocity, it will come to much the same thing.

PRISONER. Precisely, m'lud.

JEFFREYS. And in this German inflation how rapidly did the velocity increase?

PRISONER. M'lud, there are different ways of calculating it, but taking wholesale prices, seventeen times between 1921 and 1923.

JEFFREYS. I shall return to Purgatory if I have much more of this. If velocity can vary by seventeen times, then the actual stock of money, the quantity one could count at any given moment, might be multiplied in its effect on prices. One might double the money supply, but prices might increase by four, six, eight or even more times?

PRISONER. That is so, m'lud, and that is the answer to your Lordship's very significant question, how could an increase of 150 per cent in money supply support an increase of over 600 per cent, four times as great, in prices.

JEFFREYS. Are you sure that a monetary theory which has to be modified by a time lag of perhaps two years, and a change in velocity of up to seventeen times, really does offer control over inflation?

PRISONER. It does not offer the kind of simple control that some people are looking for. It is, however, the indispensable condition; increase of the money supply is the condition of inflation, restriction of the money supply, that is, stabilisation of the money supply, is the condition of ending inflation.

JEFFREYS. What makes for the changes in the velocity of circulation? Do they occur of their own, or are they the result of other forces?

PRISONER. Observations seem to show, m'lud, that changes in velocity reflect people's beliefs about the future course of prices. When people expect prices to remain steady or decline, they are content to hold money in cash, as in bank balances or deposits. Therefore the velocity of circulation will itself be steady or will tend to drop. However, people can also choose to hold cash balances, not because they think money will buy more, but because they think it may be short, that they may need it. When prices are expected to go up, people more often want to avoid holding cash, so velocity tends to accelerate. For instance, at the end of the German inflation workers not only had to be paid daily, they had to be let out before work to spend their day's wages, so as to catch the morning rather than the after-noon prices. That is an extreme example of the expectation of higher prices raising the velocity of circulation.

JEFFREYS. I think I see the point. The mechanism is not one in which the velocity of circulation is likely to contradict the effects of money supply policy; on the contrary, if the money supply increases, that tends to raise the expectation of prices and that in turn increases velocity. Equally, if the money supply is sharply restricted, that will lower price expectation and reduce velocity. Thus velocity changes tend to multiply rather than counteract the effect of monetary policy.

PRISONER. Your lordship is describing precisely what happened in the German inflation of the early 1920s on the one hand, or the American depression of the early 1930s on the other. Un-fortunately . . .

JEFFREYS. There is always an unfortunately.

PRISONER. While the principle of money supply changes and velocity changes working together applies to really major move-ments, it does not apply to those changes in money supply which are intended to break a trend. A government which is trying to throttle back inflation by restricting the money supply may well find that a continued expectation of higher prices is raising velocity and offsetting the benefits of the tight money policy. I should like here to put in another document.

JEFFREYS. Agreed.

PRISONER. It is the November 1973 issues of *The Bank Credit Analyst,* a journal published in Montreal; it is a banking journal of a scholarly character. In an article discussing the great German inflation, it points out that one of the great lessons from the German and other inflations is that once you have pushed enough money and credit into the system, rising prices can be financed by a rise in velocity even though monetary expansion is stabilised. Eventually, this creates a great squeeze and forces the government into great expansionist efforts in order to ease money and pre-empt bankruptcies.

JEFFREYS. Then the sequence is this. First you have a war, or some precedent event. Then you push up the money supply. Then prices rise. Then you try to counteract the price increases by stabilising the money supply. Then you are faced with a continuation of rising velocity which finances still higher prices, but threatens bankruptcies. You are forced to put more money in. So inflation goes on, and accelerates.

PRISONER. M'lud, that is my understanding of the process exactly. The pressure on secondary banks in Britain, the collapse of the Herstatt Bank in Germany, the distress of the U.S. banking system, including the Franklin rescue, are an example of how this stage of an inflation puts pressure on the authorities to increase the money supply, when on other grounds they would wish not to do so. It is in short much easier to avoid starting an inflation than to stop one in full career.

JEFFREYS. Did the authorities in Germany at that time see their situation in the way you are presenting it?

PRISONER. No, they did not. They were still preoccupied with their original political problem, the problem that preceded the fatal money supply decisions. When one reads the contemporary accounts, it is the questions of reparations, of the disagreement between Britain and France on reparations payments, of the French occupation of the Ruhr in early 1923, which stood out in people's minds. The reparations payments did of course damage Germany's currency in foreign exchange markets, and the occupation of the Ruhr crippled German industry. It is not at all surprising that these events caused economic collapse. It was, however, the monetary policy which ensured that the collapse should take the form of an inflation that wiped out the value of money.

JEFFREYS. I have heard that the inflation so affected the exchange rate that you could obtain a good room and dinner in a luxury hotel for less than a dollar, or a few shillings.

PRISONER. M'lud, you could. There is no doubt that the floating exchange rate, which because of the reparations Germany did not have the gold reserves to stabilise, tended to accentuate the inflation. Indeed, given fixed rates and the borrowing power to support them, it is doubtful whether such an extreme inflation could have happened.

JEFFREYS. You said that the impact of the increase in the money supply was modified by three factors. Those were the time lag, velocity and the exchange rate?

PRISONER. Yes, m'lud.

JEFFREYS. In fact all three eventually increased the inflationary effect of the increase in the money supply, did they not?

PRISONER. In fact they did, even to the point of overcoming attempts at stabilisation.

JEFFREYS. And all these depended on expectation? The time lag and the changes of velocity, as you have argued; the floating exchange rate reflected both German and foreign expectations about the future of the mark.

PRISONER. Yes, m'lud, that is true.

JEFFREYS. So we may draw two conclusions. Increasing the money supply is a most dangerous course, because of the inflation that can follow. If we face an actual inflation, we must stabilise the money supply, and must create a powerful expectation that it will remain stabilised.

PRISONER. That, m'lud, is when the next difficulty comes.

JEFFREYS. Prisoner, you are beginning to convict yourself of being an economist : whenever we see land, you push the boat back out to sea; whenever we see a clarity, you see a difficulty.

PRISONER. The difficulty, m'lud, is this. Just as in every inflation there is an increase in the money supply to begin it, so in all but the gold inflations there is later a loud complaint that there is not enough money. When inflation is in full swing, governments do not find that their citizens complain that they have too much money, but that they have too little, that trade is strangled because money is so short.

JEFFREYS. What is the reason for this? We have seen that the creation of money is a great evil, at least when created to excess, but how can it be that the act of increasing the money supply produces the complaint that the supply is too small. I do not like your paradoxes.

PRISONER. It is nonetheless so. It was so in the German inflation. It is so in our present inflation; it is true now in Britain, when the Chancellor of the Exchequer is under great pressure to increase the money supply. It is true in the United

States, where Dr Burns is trying to resist the same pressure. It was true of France in the assignat inflation; it is a necessary part of the pattern.

JEFFREYS. How so? Explain yourself.

PRISONER. The process is perhaps easiest to see in the paper money inflations, though it is clear enough in all of them. When an inflation begins, the first increase of money normally tends to stimulate trade; prices rise less rapidly than the money supply and trade moves up to the full employment level. We saw that Germany had this stage; France did, too, in the early 1790s; the world inflation in recent years had the same effect. In the second stage a momentum of prices has been created; each increase in the money supply tends to be matched by price increases equal or more than proportionate to itself; at the same time there is a resistance to further increases in the money supply by men who see what harm it is doing. M'lud, I would like now to introduce a new authority and two new concepts.

JEFFREYS. I like a good authority. I nod to a concept when I see him, but I do not choose to make a new acquaintance of one every day.

PRISONER. My authority is a nineteenth-century American historian, Professor Andrew Dickson White, the first President of Cornell University. His lectures on the French 'Fiat Money Inflation' propose a law which is called 'The law of accelerating issue and depreciation'. 'It was comparatively easy to refrain from the first issue; it was exceedingly difficult to refrain from the second; to refrain from the third and those following was practically impossible.' He compares the demand for ever larger quantities of money to the drunkard who feels the need for ever-increasing quantities of drink; in the age of drugs we might point to the same phenomenon with heroin addiction; the dose has to be increased, often to achieve a lessening effect.

JEFFREYS. And your other concept? I long to shake him by his gallows hand.

PRISONER. The concept, m'lud, is simply that of the real supply of money.

JEFFREYS. What do you mean by the real supply of money?

PRISONER. The supply of money expressed in terms of constant prices. We have seen that in inflations the velocity of circulation rises, and that simultaneously the real supply of money is falling. And indeed one sees that in each of these inflations prices do beat the money supply, that the ratio between money and transacted business turns against money. The nominal supply of money increases vastly but the real supply of money falls.

JEFFREYS. If this be so, what consequences do you derive from it?

PRISONER. That changes in the nominal supply of money determine prices; changes in the real supply of money determine economic activity. The fall in the real supply of money causes numerous economic evils. There is bound to be a shortage of liquidity in the banking system, because money is being asked to finance a disproportionate quantity of transactions. Businessmen are affected by the shortage of liquidity and respond by reducing activity. Investment and investment values fall in real terms, though in the later stages of inflation capital values usually rise in nominal terms. Unemployment rises. There is also a crisis of government finance. It has been correctly written of Germany: 'The Minister of Finance and the Governor of the Central Bank claimed in 1923 that in gold or deflated prices, money had hardly increased at all and in fact was lower than in 1913. For, typical of the later stages of hyperinflation is the inability of the Central Bank to expand real money. New issues of nominal or paper money are rejected faster than they can be printed.'

JEFFREYS. You allege, then, that it is in the nature of inflation that there should be a great surplus of nominal money and a shortage, perhaps an acute shortage, of real money.

PRISONER. That is correct, just as in earlier paper money inflations there was a lot of paper and a shortage of gold; this shortage puts great political pressure on governments. Their people feel at the same time the evil of too much nominal money and too little real money; of an inflationary crisis and a liquidity crisis. The government can see no way to increase real money except by a further increase in nominal money, though that is obviously ruinous. If there is no increase in nominal money the liquidity crisis becomes very acute; if there is an increase in nominal money it starts the whole process again and shortly has to be followed by another and bigger increase – the law of accelerating issue and depreciation.

JEFFREYS. This has been the actual process of inflation in history.

PRISONER. It has not been the case in gold inflations; but it has in all others. In Law's inflation the whole paper-making capacity of France was not sufficient to print bank notes. It is true of the assignat inflation, true in an extreme degree of the German inflation, true of the world inflation now.

JEFFREYS. Then the political reason why ceasing to add to the money supply is not a practical answer is that the real money supply will already be falling.

PRISONER. In Britain for the past year the money supply has been rising much more slowly than prices; in the United States rather more slowly. Prices have been rising less there. Both countries suffer inflation and a liquidity crisis simultaneously.

JEFFREYS. You say that governments do not start inflations for no reason; they have done it for war or for other reasons. What are these reasons now?

PRISONER. Principally the power of monopolies. Two monopolies are particularly important in this inflation: the power of the oil countries to fix the price of oil, and the power of the trade unions, who have a monopoly of the labour supply. The oil monopoly is not absolute for there are other fuels; but for some years the world has been making grossly extravagant use of cheap oil. The trade unions represent the more intractable problems of monopoly, because it is monopoly backed by social support.

JEFFREYS. In my day an association of workers to raise wages was an illegal conspiracy; I believe that is still true of an association of manufacturers to raise prices; is not the power of the trade unions the real cause of inflation?

PRISONER. M'lud, in an inflation trade unions must be regarded both as operating and as being operated on. They are not their own masters at the very time when they seem to be the masters of everyone else.

JEFFREYS. How so are they operated on? Are they compelled to go on strike?

PRISONER. They face the inflation like everyone else. Their members want to improve their earnings faster than prices, and they also want to keep their jobs. Inflation makes both these tasks more difficult, and in the end perhaps impossible. When money is stable, there need be no liquidity crisis to undermine employment; it is then quite possible to negotiate for moderate but real increases in pay. Inflation leads to unemployment; it also means that only the most powerful unions can keep their members ahead of the increase in prices.

JEFFREYS. So in your view, the unions are as much the victims of inflation as everyone else?'

PRISONER. They are indeed the victims, but they can also be the agents of inflation. The trade union leaders face the same dilemma as governments, but in a different form. Governments have the choice to stabilise the money supply, with immediately painful consequences, or to increase the money supply with ultimately catastrophic consequences. At any given point, until the final stage of inflation, the pressure of popularity works against stabilisation. The strong trade unions face a similar choice. If they use their full bargaining power they can for the moment keep their own members a jump ahead of prices. Not to do so will lose the confidence of their members. Yet if they do so then they increase proportionately the pressure for inflation, and the general expectation that inflation will actually continue. If wages increase faster than the supply of money, men will be laid off.

JEFFREYS. Surely it is in the real interest of their members that inflation should be halted.

PRISONER. M'lud it is, but for effective restraint to be achieved all trade unions would have to behave with a view to their long-term interests. Their short-term interest is more money.

JEFFREYS. I want this clear. How, in your view, do the trade unions affect inflation? A trade union makes a big wage claim, perhaps has a strike, wins a victory. Wages go up. Is that inflation?

PRISONER. No, m'lud, I think it is still a stage away from inflation. If there is no increase in the money supply, or the velocity, then these men simply make their own product dearer. Society will use less of it and their employment will decline. If their product is a necessity, which society cannot do without, then society will have less money for other goods, and employment in other areas will decline.

JEFFREYS. Then how does it lead to inflation?

PRISONER. Firstly by its effect on expectation. If major unions obtain 20 per cent increases that creates a general expectation

45

of large pay and price increases. As we have seen, when people expect inflation, changes in the velocity of circulation and the foreign exchange market may be sufficient to see that they get it.

JEFFREYS. Is the effect on expectation the main way in which trade unions increase inflation? Surely not.

PRISONER. Indeed not, m'lud. The chain of events is this. Trade unions obtain higher wages; industry has to charge higher prices; the government either has to finance these movements by increasing the supply of money or has to refuse to finance them. If the government finances them that involves a further increase in the money supply and an acceleration of inflation. If the government refuses to finance them they may be financed by an increase in the velocity of circulation, or they may be compensated for by a general fall in business activity – less business and fewer jobs at higher prices and higher wages. This is the permanent dilemma of government faced by the inflation of wages and costs, and the effect of trade union power – which is essentially a power of monopoly supply of labour – is greatly to sharpen the dilemma.

JEFFREYS. So you would say that trade unions cannot directly cause inflation, because it is the government which controls the money mechanism.

PRISONER. Yes, m'lud.

JEFFREYS. But that unions can and do use monopoly power in such a way that it is extremely difficult for any government to avoid an inflationary monetary policy. The alternative being a slump, higher unemployment and probably a lost election will follow.

PRISONER. Yes, m'lud.

JEFFREYS. Does it follow from this that incomes policies, whether voluntary or statutory, can help to relieve the pressure on monetary policy? If the unions have this powerful inflationary effect by virtually forcing a government to inflate the money supply, incomes restraint, however achieved, will reduce the pressure to inflate the money supply?

PRISONER. Yes, m'lud. The position as I see it is this. Monetary policy is the clockwork, the only clockwork which regulates the general movement of prices, which turns the hands of inflation. The government controls this clockwork. But the

46

government acts under the influence of economic and social pressures which themselves can determine whether the government will feel forced to turn the regulator to Fast or to Very Fast. Of these influences the trade unions are much the most powerful in a highly integrated modern economy, and the natural desire of their members for more money means that their influence is consistently inflationary. Incomes policies are designed to reduce that pressure and therefore such policies act in the long-term interest of the average trade unionist.

JEFFREYS. I see. The unions are like war. They are the prior question. They do not start inflation; expanding the money supply does that. But they do provide a reason for a government to expand the money supply, and they certainly provide a powerful reason for a government to fail to stabilise the money supply once inflation has started.

PRISONER. Your lordship has a wonderful grasp of this subject.

JEFFREYS. Members of the jury, you have heard what the prisoner has to say. He has told us his views of inflation, though he has not told us how he considers the matter should be mended. In this view inflation is the result of an undue increase in the money supply, and only of that. There will be precedent causes which make governments increase the money supply, wars, revolutions, perhaps even the monopoly power of trade unions. Yet, as he says, there has never been an inflation without an increase in the money supply; it is the essential condition.

Members of the jury, the prisoner further declares that once started the inflation tends to feed, if I may so put it, on the delayed effect of earlier increases in the money supply, on increases in the velocity of circulation and on any decline in the foreign exchange value of the currency, particularly when the currency is floating. He further declares that all of these forces are aggravated and accelerated by the expectation that prices will rise still further, expectations that are to a large extent self-fulfilling.

The prisoner further tells us that the inconvenience of a shortage of money in the middle of inflation, though an apparent paradox, is a natural part of the morbidity of this disease. He alleges that this is caused by prices outstripping even the largest increases in the supply of nominal money, so that the real money supply tends to fall. I was much struck by the fact that the whole German inflation was financed on a declining stock of real money.

Members of the jury, the prisoner regards the trade unions and, I would assume, other monopolies as an influence outside the monetary system, and therefore not directly causative of inflation, but nonetheless indirectly causative, and in a most powerful way. In his view they present governments with a choice between inflationary finance, which must eventually end in disaster, or an immediate crisis of liquidity, too painful for the average minister to accept even as the price of ending inflation.

Gentlemen of the jury, the prisoner is accused of being an an economist. I must direct you to acquit him of that frightful charge. I seldom direct a jury to acquit, but you will do well to remember that I expect to be obeyed.

The Court rises.

CHAPTER THREE

ROTTEN HERRINGS
AND REVOLUTION

The value of assignats, and the price of provisions differ much in different places. . . . The price of wine is at the ratio of one sou in hard cash, for four livres in assignats. On the road from Douai to Calais, ten livres in assignats were paid in a tavern for two cups of coffee. For want of hands, horses and dung, the soil is generally in a very bad state of cultivation.

The Times, March 6th, 1795

Picture of Paris. In every street, on every bridge, and in all public places, we meet with poor wretches, feeding on rotten herrings, black puddings and other unwholesome food, the smell of which is highly offensive. Amidst this afflicting spectacle blind fiddlers and ballad singers fill the air either with the 'Reveil du Peuple' or the 'Hymn of the Marseillois'. Here bands of jobbers and forestallers, throw into each other's hands, articles of trade, and raise their prices ten times above their original value, before they reach the last consumer. Alarmed at the consequences of their measures, government detaches against them brigades of soldiers who disperse them; but they assemble again at a short distance from the first place, and raise the prices of all commodities still higher. Owing to their boundless traffic, our ancient funds are sunk to a 20th of their former value, and all people of property are ruined. Robespierre, by his scaffolds, overturned the Empire, and scattered about the remnants of it; but the assignats have, since his death, accomplished the revolution and displaced everything.

Extracted from a French paper.
The Times, August 17th, 1795

Ruin and revolution are the normal consequences of inflation. The German inflation of the early 1920s prepared the way for the Nazis; the French inflation of the 1790s is interwoven with the French Revolution, and indeed with the terror – many of those guillotined were sentenced for breaches of the law of the maximum, that is, price control. The present world inflation, even at its present stage, has shaken confidence not only in individual governments, but in regimes. Even in Britain and the United States democracy is questioned as it has not been since the years of the slump and the rise of the great dictatorships.

There seem to be a number of reasons for this revolutionary tendency of inflation. To start with, inflation accelerates social change; it takes from the weak capital owner and gives to the strong; it takes from the weak trade unionist and gives to the strong. Changes of social and economic balance, which might happen anyway, happen faster than society can readily adapt to them.

Yet inflation does not only accelerate these changes, it also distorts them. In business, inflation rewards successful speculation disproportionately to successful production. In nineteenth-century Britain the great fortunes of the new men were made in industry, in coal, in steel, in tobacco, in shipbuilding, in shipping and so on. There were great property fortunes, but for the most part they were made by existing landowners as the result of development of land they already owned.

In late twentieth-century Britain the new fortunes are conspicuous in speculative finance, in property, in property related retailing, but new industrial fortunes are far from common. The reason for this is simple. Despite the risks of inflation, including the recurrent risk of liquidity crises, fortunes can be made in an inflationary time simply by skill in balancing borrowed money against appreciating assets. In a stable money period there is no automatic appreciation of assets, and they will therefore tend to rise in value only if there is an improvement in their real productivity. With stable money you have to be creative; with inflation you only have to be clever, or lucky.

So inflation not only accelerates, but diverts and disturbs

economic change. In so doing it throws up successful speculators who become the object of envy and hatred. Those whom inflation is ruining regard those who make great fortunes from inflation as the men who have ruined them. We have such figures in our own time. The United States has suffered in particular from simple fraud on a colossal scale; Mr Vesco is only the most conspicuous example.

Of the French inflation, Professor White observes, in somewhat romantic language : 'From this general distress arising from the development and collapse of "fiat" money in France, there was, indeed, one exception. In Paris and a few of the other great cities, men like Tallien, of the heartless, debauched, luxurious, speculator, contractor and stock gambler class, had risen above the ruins of the multitudes of smaller fortunes. Tallien, one of the worst demagogue "reformers", and a certain number of men like him, had been skilful enough to become millionaires, while their dupes, who had clamoured for issues of paper money, had become paupers.'

The scene that is described in Professor Golo Mann's *History of Germany since 1789* is much the same, though the inflation is in a different country and century : 'Those who were economically strong bought up the weak; German heavy industry, which even before 1914 had been concentrated in fewer hands than any other in the world, was reduced to a few empires. One of these – that of Hugo Stinnes – assumed dimensions the like of which had never been seen before, not even in America, growing as the mark depreciated. Goods were produced cheaply and cheap goods were brought onto the world market. Those who knew how to speculate, to buy and sell at the right moment, were able to live well and spent their easily-made profits freely. Shop windows glittered and turnover was high; new American dances were tried out in crowded places of entertainment while politicians drivelled contentedly about misery and lost honour. Meanwhile most people suffered real misery, the old, the pensioners, those who did not know how to speculate, and all those who worked for a wage and owned nothing.'

One sees how the successful speculator, the Stinnes, the Tallien, becomes such a focus of hatred that sober historians, writing long after the event, still write about him in highly emotional language. This resentment is felt even more strongly at the time by those who have suffered from inflation, the great majority, against those who successfully manipulate inflation to their own advantage, the small minority.

In the case of Germany, this resentment was largely turned away from the class of industrial financiers like Stinnes and came to be concentrated, as a result of Nazi propaganda, on the Jews. In Germany, as elsewhere, the Jewish community had played an important part in banking and merchanting. German Jewish banks and other businesses were among the most respectable and reliable institutions of imperial Germany. Among those successful speculators who danced so inappropriately to jazz tunes in the Berlin restaurants of 1923, there were no doubt Jews, and perhaps many Jews, to be found. Money is after all the commodity in which bankers trade, and when money explodes, more bankers than ordinary people will be able to defend themselves against it, or take advantage of it.

The result is too terrible to contemplate. The myth came to be believed that the Jews had profited from the inflation by which honest Germans – forgetting about Stinnes – had been ruined. The identification of the German Jewish community as an exploiting and alien group dates from the period of the inflation and contrasts with the ultra-patriotism of the German Jewish community in the first world war (even Freud started that war as something close to an Austro-Hungarian jingo). Although the inflation is not by any means the only root of German anti-semitism, there is a direct chain of causation from the German inflation, through the coming to power of the Nazis, to the final solution and the extermination camps. The inordinacy of money led to the inordinacy of anti-semitism.

A similar link between inflation and anti-semitism is to be found in the French Revolution. One evidence of it is to be found in a very distasteful passage in Burke's *Letter to a Member of the National Assembly*, 1791.

This is not a reason for thinking that in Britain or the United States, if things progress so far, the present inflation is likely to end in anti-semitism; that indeed seems one of the least likely of outcomes. It does, however, show what a disintegrating force in society inflation is bound to be. In this way, though not in all ways, it is worse than a great slump; a slump may leave some people still well-to-do, but it makes most people poorer in degree, the rich less rich and the poor poorer. An inflation distinguishes; some of the rich becomer richer, and some of the poor become richer too – those with strong unions. On the other hand some of the rich become poor, and some of the poor become paupers, and the number of those damaged in the end greatly exceeds the number who benefit; inflation is a perfect recipe for making people hate their neighbours.

There is also a general law of inflation that the longer and more extreme an inflation the smaller the proportion of those who can protect themselves against it. We have seen this cycle in Britain, so far as capital is concerned. When inflation is in its early stages, running, say, at below 5 per cent, most capital owners can protect themselves against it. Even at that stage, fixed interest stocks will not provide protection.

In the first stage, however, the equity investor can look with supercilious self-confidence at the troubles of the fixed interest investor. He feels himself safe, and so in the gentle inflation of the 1950s he was. Then comes a stage when the inflation is no longer supporting real expansion of the economy, but is causing increasing distress. The government resorts to price controls, and tries at least to limit the increase in the money supply. Pressures for higher wages are very strong, and confidence deteriorates.

At this point the equity investor finds that he cannot sell his shares to advantage; his gains melt away, he is making losses on some of his best investments. A table of German stock market prices during the inflation shows that equities are not a good hedge; they collapsed completely, though by the end of the inflation in November 1923, they had recovered to their post-war level of May 1919, expressed in terms of constant whole-sale prices. However, the shareholder had gone through a period when he had apparently lost nearly 90 per cent of his purchasing power on a post-war comparison and over 96 per cent on a pre-war one.

German Stock Prices

In assessing the behaviour of stocks during the inflation, the clearest picture is given after a deflating adjustment. In this case, prices are adjusted on two bases – the foreign exchange rate of the dollar (gold prices) and wholesale prices.

	Deflated by U.S. Dollar	Deflated by Wholesale Prices
Aug. 1913	100.0	100.0
May 1918	112.8	68.3
May 1919	29.7	30.6
Feb. 1920	8.5	11.9
July 1920	19.9	13.7
Jan. 1921	18.0	19.3
Sept. 1921	19.7	23.8
Oct. 1922	2.7	3.6
May 1923	8.4	11.6
Sept. 1923	22.6	22.1
Nov. 1923	39.4	32.6
Dec. 1923	26.8	21.3

Source: *The Bank Credit Analyst*, Montreal, November 1973

The falls in this table may seem less extraordinary when it is reflected that in constant gold terms, the *Financial Times* index is now at about 10 per cent of its 1968 high point; Old Consols, that is the British Government's 2½ per cent undated stock, stand at less than 1 per cent of the pre-1914 – or indeed pre-1931 – parity; the price in the market, August 1974, stands between 15 and 16, and the gold price is 17 times the pre-1914 Mint price. This was the great stock on which prudent Victorians relied for their ultimate form of security; its history can be traced back to 1751. Relatively few private individuals still hold Old Consols, but insurance companies and pension funds do hold them for their high running yield; the loss of 99 per cent of their gold purchasing power has represented a corresponding loss of real purchasing power, mainly concentrated on the elderly and on widows.

In London and Wall Street we have seen in the early 1970s that as inflation accelerates, stock market prices fall. That may not last – there seems to be a later stage, if inflation goes on, at which investors again become obsessed with real values, particularly with asset value. Yet a hedge investment which goes down as inflation goes up is the opposite of what one wants.

For a time, as it became apparent that shares would not protect their owners against inflation, property seemed to be the answer. Indeed, property in Britain has done better than shares over the last twenty years. While shares now stand at twice their nominal level of the late 1940s and early 1950s, houses, farmland and commercial properties still seem to be anywhere between ten and twenty times their immediate postwar levels, and sometimes even higher. Yet, as is painfully apparent from the present troubles of the property market and the secondary banks, property also runs out as a protection against inflation. And it has run out sharply.

A smaller group invested in works of art. They too have now begun to be overtaken by inflation. Works of art are a good store of value if wisely chosen, but they are hard to sell for a fair price when everyone is selling, or when because the real money supply is falling nobody has the money to buy.

There are a number of conclusions to be drawn from this. In the end few people benefit from inflation, though many do at the beginning. In the early days any intelligent investment prospers, and an intelligent investment backed with borrowing prospers with the benefit of gearing. In the late days even a well-considered investment is likely to fall, in terms of current purchasing power, and an investment backed with borrowed money may be squeezed out altogether.

In capital investment, from the smallest to the largest scale, inflation destroys prudent expectation. If you have assets, they may decline in value, they may even become virtually unsaleable. Yet if you have cash, you know that will rapidly become worth less, or in the extreme worth nothing. There is no right course; all roads lead to loss of value.

Yet if it destroys prudent expectation for the investor, inflation also destroys prudent expectation for everyone else. Investment is an essential function of business. In an inflation the wisest businessman may decide that all he can do is to keep afloat, avoiding any commitments which might endanger his future, continuing to produce on the stock and equipment he

55

has, and to the scale he is used to. This also destroys prudent expectation for the worker, who cannot tell what his prospects for employment are. The whole economic community slows to a pace dictated by apprehension and uncertainty.

One can trace the same pattern of loss of ability to protect oneself among trade unions. When inflation starts most people can look after their wages or salaries. Even the weakest unions do; the old-age pensioners are protected by government, or by their voting power; the prosperous retired are protected by investments, so even their income retains most if not all its purchasing power. A small group of non-unionised employees are left behind even in the first stages of inflation, and so is a larger group of fixed pension retired people. The mass voting power of the standard pensioner protects them while the retired industrial manager may be poorly protected.

A stage further on, the stage we have now reached in Britain, the weak unions can no longer keep up, nor can most managers and executives, nor in general do most of the middle class. The state old-age pension is virtually tied to the cost of living and does move up. The strong unions not only keep up, they move ahead, particularly those unions making claims on nationalised industries who do not have to fear the bankruptcy of their employer but can look to the taxpayer or to state creation of money to subsidise uneconomic wage settlements.

Yet it is certain that there comes a point in any inflation, if it is not stopped, when neither the state pension, which so far can only be adjusted administratively every half year, nor the strongest trade union, can keep ahead. It is a question of timing. In the last stages of the German inflation, ordinary cafés had a blackboard with the dollar quotation for the mark, and adjusted the price of a cup of coffee as the quotations moved. These are extreme circumstances, but we are not far from a rate of inflation which would make the whole cumbrous procedure of claim, negotiation and strike ridiculously long drawn-out compared to the actual movement of prices. The miners' bargaining power has so far actually been built up by inflation, but when wages have to be paid daily – and have to be increased daily – no trade union can protect its members, let alone actually advance their interests.

Thus all classes in society, and most members of every class,

56

are put in a position of increasing insecurity. The company director, who may be trading satisfactorily, cannot see whether he will be solvent six months ahead. The trade unionist, who may so far have maintained his standard of living or improved it, cannot see his standard of living or even necessarily his job six months ahead. This leaves aside the really unfortunate, the pensioner who sees his savings being eroded, the postman who knows that whoever else may keep up his wages, he will not. Society becomes rotted with resentment, with the belief that some other group is gaining, and with fear.

This insecurity plays into the hands of political extremists; people become more willing to support extreme solutions because they feel their own survival is at stake. The emotions of fear and resentment which inflation inevitably produces are literally killing emotions. They were the emotions of the crowd round the guillotine; they can make ordinary men regard terror as not only justified but necessary. At the same time inflation makes the rewards of life seem entirely arbitrary, the result not of contribution to society, but of expropriation from society. That undermines any social system, and promotes cynicism about society.

Every class of society is corrupted by inflation. We have seen how powerful and successful speculators come to the top. Business always involves an element of speculation, in that all business depends on an estimate of the future. Yet there is truth in the traditional distinction between business which creates real wealth and business which merely manipulates wealth in a speculative way. In periods when the first type of business has been predominant, business has in general been respected; when speculation is predominant, business is not respected.

Inflation is also very closely associated with corruption in government. The South Sea Bubble, which was a relatively minor credit inflation, was a notorious cause of corruption in the British Government. The assignat inflation was accompanied by widespread corruption in the French Assembly. The greenback financing of the American Civil War was followed by a period of extreme corruption culminating in the Presidency of Grant; the inflation in the United States during the first world war was followed by the Presidency of Harding; Watergate occurred during the most rapid inflation in modern American history.

It is natural that this should be so. In a period of stable prices it is possible for the ordinary, sensible man to plan his finances ahead; he does not expect to make a quick killing, but he can rely on maintaining his existing standard so long as he can maintain his income. He is encouraged to save because the most convenient form of saving, money, will preserve his savings in full value, until the time when he needs to use them. If he faces an emergency and his savings are not adequate, he may be able to borrow from a bank at a low rate of interest. Most of all he believes that he will be able to enjoy the honest fruits of honest work.

The opposite of all these things is true of inflation. Then many people do hope, one way or another, to make a quick gain, either in wages or by speculation. Inflation gradually pushes the whole community towards speculation, since ordinary life begins to require speculator's skills. Rapid changes in prices make it impossible to maintain a constant standard of living; for some the sacrifice is slight, a smaller car, for others it is the Sunday joint; still others cannot find a place to live. The very habit of saving is discouraged; 'save now and buy later' is changed to 'buy now and pay later'. All sections of society accept an increasingly heavy burden of debt in order to keep ahead of rising prices in their major purchases. The instability of societies in which enormous debts (Julius Caesar) jostle enormous fortunes (Crassus) is shown in the last days of the Roman Republic.

It is no wonder that in these circumstances people should become demoralised. Inflation tends to put honest men under a pressure which can open them to corruption, and tends to put dishonest men into a position where they have the money power to bribe, and often the incentive to bribe as well.

This is not a remote risk. It has been said that the German bureaucracy was incorruptible until 1922 but was not incorruptible thereafter. It has to be remembered that a bureaucracy is particularly vulnerable to inflation, and may well be demoralised by inflation even in countries where it retains its honesty. Yet this is the age when large-scale bureaucracy has become the way in which the world is governed.

58

Most bureaucrats are middle-class people; they expect and are expected to maintain middle-class standards of life. They do not expect to be rich, but they hope to be comfortable. They usually own their own houses or flats. They do not live in the most expensive quarters of London or Washington or Paris, but they do live in pleasant middle-class areas, with the costs that follow from that. Like everyone else, they may be modest about improvements in their standard of living, but are disturbed by any threat to the standard of living they have already reached, often by very hard work. Successful career bureaucrats have to work as hard as anybody.

Yet in an inflation bureaucrats are bound to suffer. They do not have strong unions; their tradition of service makes them reluctant to strike, and their work often makes striking ineffective, unless it is protracted to the point of absurdity. How long would a government statistician have to strike before the loss of his work started to compel his government to pay him more? Bureaucrats' pay is normally raised at relatively long intervals; it may then be adjusted to make up for past inflation, but is unlikely to make allowance for future inflation.

In any case government is a strong employer, and in an inflation will always be trying to discourage inflationary wage increases. It will therefore be reluctant to set a 'bad' example by giving generous, or even adequate, increases to its own servants. As a result, rising civil servants will find that the pay increases intended to reward promotion only allow them to continue to live as they have been doing already, while those who are not high fliers may feel the traditional middle-class experience, even in mild inflation, of becoming a little shabbier, accepting a small decline in living standards, year by year. In acute inflation the civil servant may go cold and hungry because his pay falls far behind; that happened in Germany.

The oppressive sense of being on a treadmill which is turning just a little faster than one can walk, of trying to run up the 'down' escalator, is indeed a common middle-class complaint in inflation, and particularly a complaint of the salaried middle class which is after all an ever-increasing proportion of the whole. It is the complaint of doctors in the British National Health Service, to the point at which it is a real threat to the future of the Service.

It is an odd thing that social theories which lead to the construction of a very large bureaucracy, often too large compared to the productive base which supports it, also tend to lead to inflation. One has to ask the question whether Fabian socialism, which presupposes a large structure of state salaried officers, can survive the demoralisation of the bureaucracy which inflation is already causing. The National Health Service may in Britain be the testing ground for that question. In Italy, with their less developed welfare system, the answer seems to be no. It is probably true that the future of democracy depends on ending inflation, but equally clearly the future of democratic state socialism will do so.

The demoralisation of the middle class is a terrible disaster to happen to a country. Not even fully excepting the trade unions themselves, the institutions of a modern industrial society are all run by the middle class. Even the affairs of the British monarchy depend on advisers and administrators who, however well born, are middle class in the sense that they are not themselves great owners of capital. The occasional business proprietor on a large scale, the occasional large landowner, provide an attractive stimulus, but the affairs of the world are in the hands of middle-class people; in practice nowadays that means people who are well educated but not rich. Even the rich have a choice nowadays; if they follow the customs of their own tribe, and lead the fashionable international life, they cut themselves off from real power. If they want to influence the world they live in, they have to pass their 'A' Levels, win acceptable degrees, go into offices and join the middle class.

There are basically two ways of beating inflation; one is to own capital, the other is to belong to a strong union. Both these means of beating inflation cease to work in the end, but at least they work for a time; they have a hope. Neither of them is open to the middle class; they are too small as individual capital owners, and their unions are too weak. Of course some of them are related by commission scales to inflation; that is true of solicitors or estate agents or stockbrokers. For them the violent oscillations of inflation will produce some nasty shocks, but at least they have incomes ultimately related to real values. The salaried middle class does not have even that safeguard.

The middle class is essential to society, whose trained

organising capacity it is. What is even worse is that the alienation of the middle class, which cannot achieve its relatively
modest ambitions of security, comfort and advancement, can
easily be turned into a middle-class hostility against the manual
working class, just as the alienation of the manual working
class becomes directed as class consciousness and class hostility
against the middle class. Because it is unjust, inflation breeds
class hatred, and on both sides.

In a modern economy the middle class, the professional
services of industry, the economy and the state, and the manual
working class, the physical operatives of industry, the economy
and the state, have interests in common which far outweigh
their conflicts. Indeed conflicts inside these classes are as significant as conflicts between them, as one sees both in manual and
in professional demarcation disputes (who tightens that bolt?
in what courts can a solicitor appear?). Yet the cultural
differences, which are based on history, locality and education,
permit political exploitation of the economic differences.

Inflation is also, after all, putting the same pressure on the
institutions of the manual working class, the trade unions. Trade
unions are seen by their members as their defence against inflation, but in the end they cannot defend their members. The
German inflation, for instance, was a disaster for the German
workers. As Professor Mann says: 'A few years previously the
German worker had won the eight-hour day and wages agreements. What use were they to him now?' Yet unions are able
to defend their members in the early stages of inflation, and in
an inflation the militant leader always seems to be right. It is
he who asks for the biggest increase, for 5 per cent when 3 per
cent has been customary, 10 per cent for 6 per cent, 20 per
cent for 12 per cent and so on. In inflation these campaigns
usually succeed, and they usually seem to be justified by
subsequent price increases which they themselves help to
cause.

Thus the strong instruments of the working class, which do
not exist for the middle class, become objects of fear and envy,
and are objects of fear and envy to members of weak unions as
well as to non-unionists. They aggravate this fear and envy by
increasingly intransigent actions, committed either by increasingly militant leaders, or by moderates aping the militants in

order to try to keep them out. This develops political tensions which are reflected by increasing hostility between political parties, at least in those countries whose party politics have a class base.

This is not a class conflict in a Marxist sense between an employing capitalist bourgeoisie and an employed proletariat. It is a class conflict between two employed classes, both dependent for their job and pensions on the same group of companies, either state or largely institutionally owned. The resentments do, however, reflect differences of economic power and differences of culture.

In considering the economic consequences of inflation it is always important to remember that it is the poorest who suffer most. In the present American inflation it is the big city poor, black and white but mostly black, who are suffering most. In Britain inflation has helped to restore homelessness as a major social problem and has sharpened the cruelties of real poverty. In the French inflation it was the very poor who ate rotten herrings; in the German inflations it was the very poor who died of cold and malnutrition. Inflation can destroy the security of all classes, but is most ruthless with the weakest.

The same holds between nations; the same inflation which makes housewives in the United States organise meatless days puts the price of food out of the reach of Bangladesh. The most valuable contribution that the major powers could make to world development would be to stabilise the level of world prices.

It cannot be denied that inflation does the work of Marxism for it, both nationally and internationally, and probably more effectively than deflation. Inflation is the great divider of societies, the sharpener of hostilities, the differentiator of interests, the enemy of moderation and the enemy of altruism. This discord pushes the extremists of the trade unions to the left and pushes the extremists of the middle class to the right. Ordinary people may start to move towards extremist political opinions, because in a major inflation democracy seems to be so helpless.

In suitable conditions, as was shown in the second world war, controls can help to limit inflation, but weak democracies tend to use direct controls not to assist in the process of ending inflation but as an alternative to ending inflation. No political power can make these controls work against the full current of inflation, yet their failure tends to discredit governments which use them. Governments are bound to be discredited if they cannot provide their citizens with the basic elements of economic stability; yet they cannot provide stability without stable prices.

These are the political consequences of inflation. Weak and brief governments, who do not really know what to do, confront the accelerating impetus of inflation, with their community increasingly divided, the country's business leadership partly discredited, the centre drifting towards despair, and the militants of right and left growing in strength. Revolutionary theories of meeting inflation are propagated and various scapegoats are pointed out : Jews, Communists, Fascists, grain merchants, the agents of foreign powers, forestallers, Herr Stinnes, Mr McGahey or whom you will. Even Shakespeare blamed high food prices on the 'farmer, that hang'd himself on the expectation of plenty'. As the inflation drives on, it becomes so intolerable that almost any solution that will reimpose authority on money is contemplated. I remember a Brazilian civil servant, who served the old democracy and the new dictatorship, saying to me, 'If it happens to you, you will find you think differently when inflation is 10 per cent a month from the way you do when it is 10 per cent a year.' It is no wonder that Brazil, like Chile, China, Hungary, the Soviet Union or France, joined the group of nations in which revolution was caused by or accompanied by inflation.

These revolutions all tended towards authority; indeed it is arguable that in the French Revolution both the coming to power of the Jacobins and Napoleon, both the terror and the empire, owed their existence as much to the economic and social pressures of inflation as to any other cause. Yet inflation is relatively impartial; it is a threat to the survival of any regime; it destroyed even the Marxist regime of Allende's Chile. Of the five European regimes with the worst inflation records in 1973 – Greece, Spain, Yugoslavia, Portugal and Finland – four were authoritarian. That did not prevent two of them, Portugal and Greece, from falling in the following year, for reasons which included inflation as well as foreign wars. In the case of Portugal the colonial campaign in Africa greatly helped inflation along.

Why then do governments inflate, when it so clearly presents a fatal threat at least to them and perhaps to their systems? There seem to be several reasons : they believe inflation will help economic expansion; they do not know how to avoid inflation consequent on excessive wage settlements; they believe that inflation will help them to win elections (usually false) or that deflation would ensure that they lost them (possibly true?); they suffer from world inflation, from a general excess growth of the world money supply; they do not wish to raise taxes to pay fully for their own very large expenditure, particularly on social services, defence, or even, as now in Britain, on supposedly anti-inflationary subsidies. Basically, however, governments inflate, whether they are democratic or authoritarian, because they are under intense political pressures, have no confidence that any theory of the causation of inflation is correct, do not know what to do, and do not see what else they can do.

In theory, government expenditure, however high, cannot cause inflation if it is fully covered by taxation. In practice, high government expenditure tends to be inflationary, partly because governments seldom do cover it fully by taxation and resort in some degree to credit creation. There is also in most government transfer payments a Robin Hood element, taking from the rich to give to the poor. Unfortunately the rich tend to use money to acquire or maintain capital assets, while the poor use money to spend in a way that uses current economic resources. Defence expenditure has the same effect on resources, except that it does not of itself attack capital which has already been saved. However, the building of a tank does use real resources, does create spending power in the hands of the people who build it, and the tank does nothing to satisfy spending power. You cannot eat it, put it in your house or use it to quieten the children.

It would remain true that if strict monetary discipline were followed, no amount of defence spending would cause inflation; it would merely have its direct proportionate effect on other claims on the economic resources available to satisfy consumer demand. Yet when one recognises the close association between war and inflation, one cannot be surprised that the very high levels of defence expenditure by major powers in the 1960s was associated with the development of world inflation. Indeed the Vietnam War more than any other factor forced the United States to suspend convertibility of the dollar, *de facto* in 1968, *de jure* in 1971; that began the latest and most vicious phase of the world inflation.

Inflation obviously creates pressures for more government expenditure, partly because the government's purchases, like everyone else's, cost more, but partly also because inflation makes people careless about money. They become drunk with too many noughts. Stable money is difficult to earn, but is worth earning and is cared for; inflationary money is easier to come by (not necessarily by earning it); it is not worth keeping and is wasted.

Taxation policy also faces inflationary problems. The left-ward drift of the early phases of inflation – a sharp rightward reaction often sets in later – encourages attempts, which are often disappointing to their authors, to raise taxation to in-ordinate heights. At present in Britain all investment income above a total taxable income of £20,000 pays tax at 98 per cent – a ludicrously extreme encouragement to wasteful capital spending by the rich. At the same time inflation itself pushes an increasing number of people, whose incomes may even be rising less rapidly than prices, into higher tax brackets. It has been suggested that all taxes should be indexed and the levels at which they apply should be allowed to float upwards. Yet that would actually remove one of the most powerful counter-inflationary forces in the economy, that inflated incomes not only pay more tax, but more tax proportionately.

There is also a growing problem of tax avoidance (lawful) and tax evasion (direct cheating). In the 1970s we have already seen a Prime Minister of France and a President of the United States run into serious political trouble because of the accusation that they had minimised their tax payments. In Britain a genera-tion ago there was a social consensus that taxes ought to be paid willingly as a contribution to the proper cost of running the state; a generation of very high taxation has watered this down to a consensus that taxes legally due should be paid; already there is a fringe of outright illegality, and there must be reason to fear that another few years of inflation and high taxation would destroy the average Englishman's law-abiding attitude toward his taxes, and with it a substantial part of the taxing capacity of the government.

Inflation is very unjust to women; they feel and express as voters a much sharper resentment at rising prices than is common among men. This is partly because men receive the wage increases and women pay the price increases. In practice, inflation usually expands the free spending money of men quite rapidly. If a man gets £50 a week in his pay packet and pays £30 to his wife for the housekeeping, he is left with £20 for himself. If he receives a 20 per cent increase to match a 20 per cent increase in the cost of living, his take-home pay, subject to variations in his tax position, will go up by £10. Even if he splits the £10 equally between the housekeeping and himself, which is more generous than many husbands would be, he is awarding himself a 25 per cent rise, which will take him ahead of the cost of living, and giving his wife a rise of only 16.6 per cent, which leaves her behind the cost of living. In not a few cases the husband, at least for some months, keeps the whole of the £10 for himself.

Inflation has always had the same monetary causes and the same social consequences. There is no inflation which has not started with an increase in the money supply; there is no inflation which has not ended with a corruption of society, proportionate only to the degree of the inflation itself. It corrupts and weakens every social institution; it makes every member of society feel himself to be the victim of every other member of society; it sets class against class. It makes governments weak and unsure of themselves; it has in recent history destroyed more lawfully constituted governments than any other force except war itself.

This is because all inflation is by its nature both inordinate and unjust; in the end it destroys wealth, but from the start it makes a great transfer of wealth, both between classes and inside classes, which does not reflect work or merit or economic contribution, but skill in speculation, luck, militancy or industrial bargaining power. It makes the whole economic system seem unjust and the whole political system seem ineffective. It makes men take short views; when money is good men plant oaks, when it is bad they can at best plant cabbages. It makes men corrupt, both by impoverishing them arbitrarily and by enriching them arbitrarily.

Money does not make a society strong or just, prosperous or wise. These things require other institutions and exertions. For that matter blood, however well it circulates, does not make a man strong or wise; those are qualities of muscle and mind which he may or may not possess. Yet a disease of blood or a disease of money can corrupt the physical or social body; bad money will mean that a society becomes weak and unjust, poor and confused. Good money will not bring the good society, but bad money will absolutely certainly destroy it.

CHAPTER FOUR

THE CASE FOR GOLD

The individualistic Capitalism of today ... presumes a
stable measuring rod of value and cannot be efficient –
perhaps cannot survive – without one.

John Maynard Keynes
Tract on Monetary Reform, 1923

The argument that convinced me of the case for gold was that
it worked. We are in the middle of a world inflation which is
described by the Organisation for Economic Co-operation and
Development as 'unprecedented' for all its members and as 'intolerable' for Japan, which at the beginning of 1974 had an
inflation rate of 24.5 per cent. Since 1968 the link with
gold in the world monetary system – the convertibility of
the dollar into gold – has been broken in fact, and since 1971
has been broken completely. That has been the period in which
the world inflation has accelerated from unsatisfactory but
tolerable to unprecedented and intolerable levels.

Yet it is not to the pre-1968 Bretton Woods compromise that
one would look for the basic proof of the relationship between
a gold standard and price stability. There are much longer runs
of historic experience to be examined, under conditions much
closer to those of a perfect gold standard.

First of all one should examine British experience. From the
restoration of King Charles II in 1660 down to the outbreak of
the first world war Britain operated on an unqualified gold
standard. There was a debt repudiation in the reign of Charles
II, which need not be taken into account, and suspension of
convertibility by the Bank of England from 1797 to 1821, which
was made necessary by the war with France. However, from
1661 to 1913, with the exception of the Napoleonic period,
there was full internal and external convertibility into gold, so
complete that all other forms of money can be regarded simply

Prices since 1661 (1661 = 100)*

Figures for each decade are along a horizontal line: e.g. that for 1667=88, for 1944=195.

	0	1	2	3	4	5	6	7	8	9
166–		100	103	101	96	96	92	88	88	84
167–	85	84	81	80	86	92	88	81	82	87
168–	85	82	82	80	81	83	84	74	74	73
169–	75	76	75	78	87	87	89	90	95	98
170–	85	74	73	70	73	66	75	65	68	79
171–	90	100	75	72	76	77	73	70	69	72
172–	75	74	68	66	70	72	75	71	73	77
173–	70	65	66	63	65	66	64	69	67	66
174–	74	80	73	70	62	63	69	67	70	71
175–	70	67	69	67	67	68	68	81	78	74
176–	73	70	70	74	75	78	79	81	80	73
177–	74	79	87	88	86	84	84	80	87	82
178–	81	85	86	95	93	89	88	87	90	87
179–	92	90	90	95	101	109	114	110	110	118
180–	157	169	129	115	119	138	136	138	151	157
181–	153	152	175	180	155	141	127	140	144	128
182–	115	105	101	104	106	115	102	102	97	95
183–	95	97	95	93	97	97	107	102	103	113
184–	111	105	96	91	94	95	95	100	87	82
185–	82	79	82	97	108	108	108	110	96	100
186–	104	100	104	105	103	102	104	102	100	93
187–	95	100	111	110	105	102	100	95	88	85
188–	89	86	88	88	82	76	72	70	73	73
189–	76	75	71	71	64	62	63	64	68	73
190–	79	75	75	75	72	75	81	84	76	80
191–	84	86	91	91	91	116	146	193	207	222
192–	270	167	141	139	150	146	136	131	129	124
193–	104	89	86	85	103	103	106	110	113	113
194–	152	205	195	177	195	191	191	205	219	227
195–	234	251	269	273	276	287	301	312	319	319
196–	322	333	347	354	365	379	396	404	425	446
197–	474	513	545	595						

*Linked index. Main sources: Mitchell and Deane, Abstracts of British Historical Statistics, and Department of Employment, British Labour Statistics Historical Abstract 1886-1968.
Basic series: Schrumpeter-Gilboy price index 1661-1697 (1697=100) and 1696-1823 (1701=100); Rousseaux price indexes 1800-1923 (1865 to 1885= 100); Sauerbeck Statist price indexes 1846-1938 (1867 to 1877=100); DE index of the internal purchasing power of the pound 1914-1968 (1963=100).
Series rebased on 1661=100 using the multipliers: 1697=100; 0.9174: 1701= 100, 0.7399; 1865-1885=100, 0.8679; 1867-1877=100, 1.0761; 1963= 100, 3.5417.

Source: *The Economist*, July 13, 1974

as convenient transferable receipts for gold. Gold was money and money was gold.

During the pre-Napoleonic period from 1661 to 1796, according to a most valuable table of prices compiled by the *Economist,* the low point of prices occurred in 1743, at an index figure of 62 against 100 for 1661. The high was 114 in 1796, shortly before the suspension of convertibility. In the post-Napoleonic period, from 1822 to 1913, leaving out 1797 and 1821 when there was not convertibility for the whole year, the low was again 62 in 1895, and the high was 115 in 1825, again close to the non-convertible period. The high of the wartime inflation of the Napoleonic War was 180.

There must be some reservation about price indices compiled over such a long period, but the high degree of stability they show is not illusory. Prices in Britain were very stable for the two hundred and fifty years after the Restoration, with the exception of the Napoleonic period. It is quite plausible that prices were about 10 per cent lower in 1913 than in 1661; there is nothing in what we know of the economic circumstances of those two periods to contradict it. Prices were very low in the middle 1740s and the middle 1890s.

Yet what these figures suggest is that the British price system in this period was not only stable but had a strong tendency to return to an equilibrium point. In fact the choice of 1661 as the base year slightly obscures this pattern, for 1661 was still a year of some political excitement and therefore of relatively high prices. If one takes the first year of each decade from 1670 on, one has a better picture of the degree of stability (again excluding the non-convertible years): 85, 85, 75, 85, 90, 75, 70, 74, 70, 73, 81, 92, 95, 111, 82, 104, 95, 89, 76, 79, 84. Of these twenty-one years, twelve, including the first five and the last four, fall into the range from 75 to 90; four fall below 75; five rise above 90. It seems clear from this that there was a equilibrium range towards which prices tended to return.

This long period of history cannot be dismissed as uneventful. Though it excludes the Napoleonic War, it includes Marlborough's wars, it includes one successful and three unsuccessful attempts to change the British regime, it includes the industrial revolution, it includes the impacts of the American War of Independence and the American Civil War, it includes the creation of the British Empire, virtually the whole of it, it even includes the creation of the trade unions, and it includes the development of modern parliamentary democracy on mass suffrage. Nor was it a period of long-term economic depression or of failure to increase wages. Industrially it was a most creative period in British history and real wages rose firmly, though not without interruption. Yet during the whole of this period the British price system beat like a steady pulse, affected by economic and political events but with a strong natural tendency to return to normality. One only has to contrast that period of centuries with what now happens to prices in a year or so, to see how great a benefit we have lost, whatever the reasons for losing it. Our price indexes now rise by nearly 20 per cent in a year, compared to the 10 per cent decline in the 252 years from 1661 to 1913, or to the one per cent decline in the 240 years from 1670 to 1910.

One should not, however, look at British experience alone. In the monetary history of the United States we have shorter runs and more monetary experimentation. From 1879 to 1914 the dollar was convertible into gold at a fixed ratio specified by law and maintained in practice. Chart 62 of Friedman and Schwartz, *A Monetary History of the United States*, shows the high degree of stability of wholesale prices in that period, fully comparable to the stability in Britain.

The contrast between earlier periods and our own is the more striking because our weapons of economic analysis are now so much more powerful than theirs were. Apart from developments of economic theory, some of which may of course be mistaken, we have a capacity to collect statistics, and process them through computers, which gives us a vastly greater knowledge of the progress of our economic system. Yet the government of King Charles II (whom Burke rather harshly described as 'dissolute, false, venal, and destitute of any positive good quality whatsoever, except a pleasant temper, and the manners of a gentleman'), itself often bankrupt, certainly corrupt, with no coherent economic theory, a century before Adam Smith, using quill pens, was able after the Restoration to start a quarter-millennium of price stability, while we are despairingly coming to believe that inflation is an unavoidable curse of mankind. If medicine had progressed in the same way as economics, London would have been quite free of plague in 1665, but now plague would be endemic, and world-wide.

There can be no real doubt that it was the gold standard which produced this extraordinary price stability. The correlation is perfect; there is no period of history, except for the recognisable gold inflations in which new mined or plundered gold was too rapidly increasing the gold stock, in which successfully maintained gold standards have not been accompanied by long-term price stability, either nationally or internationally. Even the gold inflations are mild and long-term, not explosions of inflation. The record of currencies not in any way linked to gold is one of almost consistent inflation, often explosive. All gold standard money has been good money; all non-gold money, if totally divorced from a metallic standard, has proved to be bad money. Why then did the pound not suffer more rapid inflation between 1931 and 1971? Because for most of that period the pound was fixed to the dollar and the dollar was convertible into gold. We have not had a satisfactory gold standard since August 1914, but with brief intervals we have had some continuing gold discipline down to 1971, despite the changes and experiments of the intervening period.

The question that has to be considered is how gold achieves these, to us, astonishing results. Gold is not magic. Because of its long association with money, gold does have a symbolic hold upon the human imagination. This can make it politically more powerful, or it can repel people. But as *Little Arthur's History of England* puts it, 'you must know that gold is only useful to help people in exchanging one useful thing for another'.

The answer is in essence quite simple. Gold is indeed the conclusive proof of the monetarist case, though not all monetarists believe in gold. Professor Friedman, the leading monetarist, believes that the ideal policy would be to ensure that the money stock was constant but gradually increasing. A money stock which is gold, or is limited by relationship to a gold base, naturally fulfils these conditions. The gold stock will neither diminish nor increase as the result of human action, except through industrial use of new mining, and those will always form only a small proportion of the existing world stock of gold.

Obviously it is possible for the authorities of an individual country to adopt monetary policies which follow the Friedman doctrine, and some monetarists argue that gold is an unnecessary complication because you can achieve the right policies without gold. Such policies do tend to correct inflation, but they suffer from two important disadvantages.

The first is that monetary policy does not have the same effect on expectation that gold does. For instance, during the French inflation, the actual plates for printing assignats were publicly destroyed in order to convince the public that new assignats were not going to be created. Even that did not work. A modern government makes decisions about monetary policy which only a tiny minority understand, and not all of those believe will be carried through. Therefore a strict money supply policy has a long time-lag before it can be seen to be a consistent part of government policy. The gold commitment is not itself unchangeable, but it is seen immediately and its nature is generally understood. A government which goes on gold makes a statement to its people that in future the nation will have to earn real money, that the government and individuals will both have to pay their way in the world in the hardest of hard currencies, that the money supply will be limited.

The second advantage of gold is that it is the only way to secure sound monetary policies for the whole world at once. Professor Friedman is not going to be able to persuade all governments, or even all major governments, to control their money in the same way. Gold not only automatically provides the ideal money supply policy – or something close to it – but also provides it as a world money supply. This is all the more important as it is now a world inflation which we have to bring under control.

Supposing one were trying to set up a world money system to provide for economic stability, including price stability – and there is no stability without price stability – its characteristics would be that the money supply should be constant, that it should gradually increase, that it should not be open to individual governments to add to it, that it should not be open to unregulated credit markets, such as the Euro-currency market, to add to it, that it should be widely acceptable. Perhaps one would add that this new system must be objective rather than subjective, so that it would not be open to political pressure; perhaps also that it should be permanent, that the form of the money itself should be immutable. One might, in working out the ideal terms for a world currency system designed to bring to an end an age of inflation, reach such conclusions as these. One would have invented the gold standard.

Gold has worked historically and meets, in a way no paper system does, the theoretical requirements of a stable world monetary system. There are difficulties to be discussed, but they will be taken later. Yet it has two further advantages, both very important.

The first is that it is concrete and unchangeable, not abstract and changeable. All other currency systems, except other metallic ones, depend on the authority of the issuing government. That authority is both abstract and changeable. All human organisations perish over time. The Roman Catholic Church is as old as the Christian era, save for some fifty years; that is a religious organisation, against which the gates of Hell shall not prevail, but secular organisations seldom have that length of life. Democratic governments change at elections, dictatorships change by intrigue or force. However powerful the government, its currency is only a promise to pay on behalf of a temporary authority, a promise to pay limited by a temporary capacity to pay. There is no authority now which will pay on the promise of Alexander, or Julius Caesar, Louis XIV, Peter the Great, Napoleon or Hitler; they were powerful men in their time but no bank now will cash their cheques. Yet take a gold ingot which was once in their treasuries and you can obtain value for it anywhere in the world. The permanence and universality of gold give it an authority as money which no other money has.

There is also an advantage that may prove in the end to be the crucial one. I argued earlier that changes in the nominal money supply control prices, but that changes in the real money supply control the level of economic activity. This must logically be so. If the supply of money doubles and prices double, then the expansive effect on demand of the increase in money is precisely counteracted by the contracting effect of the increase in prices. If, on the other hand, the money supply doubles, but prices increase by less than that, then there will be spare money to be spent, and that will call for further business activity.

The evidence from France in the 1790s, from Germany in the early 1920s and from the world inflation now, is that inflation goes through two major stages (in fact the phases of inflation are more complicated than this, but the two stages represent the vital distinction). In phase one, the money supply increases faster than prices; this is possible because there is still some slack in the economy, inflationary expectation is still weak, governments are as yet unafraid of increasing the money supply. In these circumstances business activity improves because the increase in the nominal money supply is also an increase in the real money supply.

In the second phase prices tend to increase faster than the money supply. We have seen that this presents governments with a dilemma which is actually insoluble in orthodox neo-Keynesian terms. If the government pursues a strict monetary policy then the real money supply is very sharply deflated, and this produces a slump. If the money supply is further inflated, then the inflationary cycle goes a stage further. In the final stages of an inflation governments may actually be unable to keep up. So-called stagflation and slumpflation are the inevitable reflection of the progressive divergence between a rising nominal and a falling real supply of money.

In this situation gold is not only the best way of dealing with the inflation; it is also the best way of dealing with the slump. It is known that the real world stock of gold cannot be artificially increased; that is a powerful corrective to inflationary expectation. It is also known that the real world stock of gold cannot be artificially reduced; that is a powerful corrective to deflationary expectation. Gold is often thought of as an inherently deflationary monetary system, because it is so easy to see how it limits inflation by limiting the money supply. In fact gold does not naturally lead to deflation; it was certainly not gold which caused the great slump, but a mismanagement of the United States money supply not consequent on gold or gold movements. The natural tendency of gold is to prevent rapid alteration of the money stock, and therefore to inhibit inflation and deflation alike.

If, in the immediate future, we have to face a world slump or severe depressions in individual countries, it will be because the monetary authorities are trying to restrain inflation while prices are still rising. The only result can be a sharp contraction of the real money supply. The right way to correct this tendency to world slump, which is itself inherent in a world inflation, is to change to a money supply which is known for sure to be constant.

This can be shown by the behaviour of interest rates. The record of stable long-term interest rates under the gold standard is comparable to the stability of prices. In the 157 fully convertible years between 1731 and 1913, British interest rates on undated government stocks stayed with marked consistency in the range between 3 and 4 per cent. In twenty of those years interest rates were below 3 per cent throughout the year; in eleven of those years interest rates were at 4 per cent or above; the highest recorded rate was 5.7 per cent in 1782. In 136 of the years long-term interest rates were between 3 and 4 per cent for part or all of the year, usually for all of it. The comparable stock now yields nearly 16 per cent (August 1974).

If we suppose a government which decided to pursue a policy of close restriction of the money supply, what would be the effect on interest rates? They would unquestionably rise. The market would expect a liquidity crisis, short-term interest rates would rise sharply, long-term interest rates would rise sympathetically and would only start to fall when it was seen that any forced sales of stocks had been completed, and that the rate of inflation had actually started to fall.

What would happen to interest rates if instead of restricting the supply of money, without changing the character of the money, the same government followed the same policies, but with the addition of a return or an intention to return to the gold standard? Unquestionably, long-term interest rates would fall. At present many people are content to hold gold in the form of bullion, which cannot yield interest. A government-guaranteed gold stock with interest, if issued or converted by a government with a good record for avoiding default, ought to yield something around the historic 3 to 4 per cent rate for undated British government securities.

No doubt it would take some time for confidence to develop; yields on British undated stocks would not fall immediately from over 15 to under 5 per cent, but they would fall, and given the backing of balanced financial policies they would go on falling to something around the traditional rate. Even now the United States could probably float a gold loan at the traditional rates, and could perhaps borrow long-term on a gold pledge at 3 per cent.

Interest rates on bonds redeemable in gold tend to approximate to interest rates on farm land. Land and gold are indeed closely linked; they are two permanent economic factors, both of limited availability. Land is less convenient than bullion in so far as it is not portable, and is therefore in currency terms not liquid. If, however, bullion is regarded as equivalent to liquid land, and receives no interest, gold loans and land receive interest in compensation for the reduction of liquidity involved in their ownership. Land has traditionally been dealt in at 20 to 25 years purchase of the gross rent, equivalent to a 3 to 4 per cent rate of interest, after allowing for the expenses of the landowner. Inflation, which has pushed up paper interest rates, has conversely pushed down the interest on land, as a real asset.

Thus the view that it comes to the same thing to have a strict monetary policy or a gold policy falls down on the interest rate argument. A strict monetary policy does not of itself tend to equilibrium or to low interest rates; it tends to high interest rates and to slump. It is preferable to further inflation through easy money, but that is all one can say. Gold tends to lower interest rates, and to re-establish equilibrium.

Of course, if this fall in nominal interest rates were also a fall in real interest rates it might be highly inflationary. It is not. In Britain the current rate of inflation is 19 per cent or thereabouts. The real rate of interest on undated government securities (now 16 per cent) is therefore approximately minus 3 per cent per annum, even for those who enjoy it tax free. In other words the government charge 3 per cent per annum for the privilege of lending them money. A 4 per cent rate of interest on a gold standard undated government security would be 4 per cent nominal and 4 per cent real. Nominal interest rates would drop by 12 per cent, but real interest rates, in terms of constant money, would rise by 7 per cent, from 3 per cent negative to 4 per cent positive.

This change cannot be achieved by any manipulation of paper money whatsoever, because the expectation of gold cannot be won by paper money. It is obvious that such a change is beneficial to the lender. He is now being robbed of money by the depreciation of the currency, and there is no way in which he can protect himself. He would be restored to a position in which he would be modestly but genuinely paid for the use of his money, and would be able to get it back at its full gold value. The whole problem of pensions would become easier to solve and there would obviously be a strong encouragement to save. Nobody really knows what the relationship of actual saving to the true rewards of saving is, but what influence stability has on saving must be favourable.

The borrower would seem at first sight to lose by the bargain. At present he borrows bad money at a high rate, expecting to repay it in worse money. Then he would borrow good money, admittedly at a lower rate, and would have to repay it in equally good money. He would borrow so many ounces of gold and be obliged to repay an equal number of ounces of gold.

Yet different borrowers would be affected in different ways. The speculator would suffer because there would be no automatic deterioration of money to raise the prices of the commodity or property he purchases with the loan. The trader and the industrialist are, however, less concerned than the speculator with long-term changes in capital value, and more concerned with the proportion of borrowing costs to gross margins of profit. They are also concerned with keeping the interest penalty for an error of judgement as low as possible.

If a manufacturer borrows from his bank at 15 per cent, he has to be able to see a profit on top of that 15 per cent inside the period in which he is planning to use the money. Even in an inflationary boom that may be difficult. In an inflationary slump it may be impossible. Over three years at compound interest of 15 per cent, £100 borrowed becomes more than £150; in five years more than £200. A businessman can therefore run into really serious difficulties in relatively short periods if he is borrowing at these rates of interest. At 5 per cent compound interest, £100 takes nine years to reach £150, a period which gives a businessman time to correct an error, and makes a minor misjudgement of the market relatively inexpensive.

Inflation in general makes business more difficult to transact, because it makes it more difficult to predict. High nominal interest rates accentuate the penalty on business errors. Small but stable profits encourage business expansion more than higher but uncertain profit expectations.

In practice, therefore, businessmen engaged in making or selling tend to think in terms of nominal rather than of real rates of interest. They will be more deterrred by high nominal, but negative real rates of interest, than by low nominal rates which are also positive in real terms. Speculators must think differently, but a switch of willingness to use money from speculation to production is obviously desirable in itself.

This point is of great importance. The characteristic of a gold system is that it has an automatic tendency to revert towards price and interest rate equilibrium. This discipline is exercised through a constant world money supply; for the individual country it is exercised through the penalty of losing gold or having to borrow in circumstances of trade deficit. A gold standard therefore also naturally tends towards equilibrium of trade, and universality of prices.

In particular, gold is ideally suited to the final stages of inflation, because it at the same time counteracts four destructive forces : the rise in prices, the fall in the real money supply, the rise of interest rates (at the peak of the German inflation interest rates were paid of 200 per cent a month) and the non-acceptability of money. In these circumstances a gold policy is the most favourable policy for restoring a higher level of economic activity and raising employment. In slumpflation gold is specific to counteract not only the inflation but also the slump.

What then are the objections? There are important technical objections which have to be considered, but there are also basic philosophical and economic objections. For Britain it means abandoning the overriding post-war priority to full employment. That does not mean abandoning the objective of full employment; indeed in present circumstances a gold standard policy could well become the only way to maintain high levels of employment.

It was clearly stated in the 1944 White Paper on Employment Policy: 'Action taken by the Government to maintain expenditure will be fruitless unless wages and prices are kept reasonably stable. This is of vital importance to any employment policy, and must be clearly understood by the public.' In the *Economic Journal*, 1943, Keynes took the same point: 'Some people argue that a capitalist country is doomed to failure because it will be found impossible in conditions of full employment to prevent a progressive increase in wages. . . . Whether this is so remains to be seen. The more conscious we are of this problem, the likelier we shall be to surmount it.' The weakness of the position can be judged from the uncharacteristic feebleness of Keynes' last sentence. In fact therefore, on Keynes' or the White Paper's assumptions, the full employment standard has already been totally undermined by the failure to keep wages and prices reasonably stable.

What has to change is the degree of priority. We have tried to operate the economy with a constant high level of employment as an absolute, around which everything else – prices, money supply, external trade – was supposed to vary. This was made to work until the late 1960s by a compromise between full employment policies and a commitment not to devalue in terms of the dollar, while the dollar was still linked to gold. This compromise resulted in the stop-go policies of this period, which themselves tended to prevent runaway inflation. In itself, however, the full employment standard has no tendency to bring the economy into equilibrium; on the contrary, while full employment can flow from the successful management of an equilibrium system, a full employment standard system as such is inherently inflationary and therefore self-destructive.

We do in any case have to abandon the economic model of the 1944 White Paper, unless there is a return to the conditions of prolonged world slump which produced it. The 1944 system uses government expenditure to regulate the economy; the expenditure is not covered by taxation or genuine borrowing out of savings and therefore increases the money supply, and increases economic activity through the Keynesian multiplier. In deflationary circumstances this works, because an increase in the nominal money supply will increase the real money supply; it continues to work in conditions of stable or gently rising prices; in rapid inflation it ceases to work, because by then the government, while continuing to control the nominal money supply, has lost control of the real money supply.

In American terms the objection to gold has been put with

elegant brevity by Professor Friedman. Under a gold system the stock of money of an individual country becomes a dependent, not an independent variable, since under a gold system the stock of money responds to changes in the balance of payments. This is why monetarists often reject gold. They see money as the control system of the economy; they want to keep it under their control. Under a gold system the stock of money, allowing for borrowing and a certain amount of management, is dependent on external trade. If there is an overall external deficit the stock of money contracts – or has to be contracted in order to restore or maintain international confidence – and prices and employment tend to fall; if there is an overall surplus the stock of money expands and prices, employment and wages tend to rise.

There is a psychological resistance to accepting the idea of gold. It is alarming to human nature, this icy shock of facing the absolute, though most people are perfectly happy to be flown across the Atlantic by an automatic rather than a human pilot. The absolute is itself not uniformly favourable; it is much more comfortable for a strong economic country to attach itself to an automatic self-equilibriating system than for a weak one.

Yet when one compares the systems one sees that the objective gold system provides real advantages over the subjective paper one. Gold provides a constant or slowly increasing world stock of money; paper does not. Gold makes world inflation impossible; paper makes world inflation inevitable. Gold forces countries to face the realities of their economic position, and at an early stage; paper allows countries to delude themselves about their position until they have stocked up trouble. Gold leaves little room for economic manipulation for electoral purposes; paper tempts governments to buy votes by inflation. Gold provides stable and continuous objectives for business; paper produces wild fluctuations in business conditions.

Dr Norbert Weiner's classical work on *Cybernetics*, the theory of communication systems, first established the characteristics of effective and ineffective control systems. A gold system is a self-equilibriating system operating on a constant world money supply, in the same way that a self-equilibriating navigational system can operate on magnetic North as its stable measuring rod. Managed money systems all have the characteristic of extreme oscillations of over-correction which mark the defective cybernetic system, and because they lack a stable point of reference, they are logically defective; you cannot read a map if North is mobile. One might think that no one dependent on the British money supply in the last decade would now prefer subjective judgement to automatic objectivity.

What is it one is putting first if one opts for gold? It is the equilibrium of the whole world monetary system. That in itself does not solve the economic problems of the world, or the economic problems of individual nations, but it does go as far as money can go to create conditions in which nations can try to solve their own problems according to their own political and economic systems. Certainly it does not confront them with the problems of wild instability of world money which we now face. Over any long period of time this instability is likely to produce higher average rates of unemployment, as well as more distress, than gold did or would do.

Yet this instability is inevitable if the world depends, as it now does, on multiple, separately managed national currencies. We now have no world currency – unless S.D.RS. are called such – but exchange dubious national promissory notes which are all more or less over-issued. These promissory notes are not even all regulated by the nation concerned; on top of the national credit inflations we have the credit inflation of the Euro-currency markets. Nothing could be more certain than that in such a system most nations will somewhat inflate, and some nations and the Euro-currency markets will grossly inflate, the issue of these untrustworthy tickets; that could be predicted, it has happened and it is happening. A world money supply which is the sum of inflated national money supplies can itself only produce world inflation, with steep swings into slump when inflated prices outstrip inflated issues of currency. After two and a half thousand years we have produced the most divided, the least controlled, the most untrustworthy and the most dangerous currency system the world as a whole has known.

This has all been done with the sincere intention of increasing the welfare of mankind through economic growth. There is of course a genuine question about the optimum rate of increase in the money supply to finance the optimum rate of economic growth. There is also a question about the optimum rate of economic growth, and perhaps that needs to be looked at first.

In the post-war period a purely statistical approach to economic growth has often been followed. That was dangerously misleading, partly because the statistics were often wrong (Communist statistics were often mere propaganda, or the summary of false statements, made for self-interested reasons). Even when the statistics were right they over-emphasised rapid industrial growth relative to the general development of the society. As a result Japan appeared to be much the most successful economy of the world, at a time when lop-sided industrial growth at an astonishingly rapid rate was causing almost every type of consequential problem of social disorientation, big city slums, pollution and so on. The most succesful nation by the standard of the 1960s was rapidly destroying her own civilisation. Most observers are now agreed that a slower but better balanced economic development, with more attention to social development, would have served Japan better. Inordinate statistical growth was good for political speeches, but not good for people.

Balanced growth and a conservationist attitude towards nature and natural resources are almost certainly better suited than maximum growth to the real welfare of human beings. Balanced investment is more productive than Stalinist investment drives. Unlimited paper credit tends to finance and encourage both speculation and in favourable conditions exactly the kind of exorbitant growth that has now rightly come under suspicion.

The ideal would probably therefore be that the world's money stock should grow by about $3\frac{1}{2}$ per cent per annum, a reasonable approximation to the world's annual potential for sound development. The gold stock will not increase at that rate. New mined gold in South Africa and the Soviet Union, less industrial use, might at best increase the gold stock by something of the order of 1 per cent, but the rate cannot be calculated, as it depends on facts we do not know about Russian production, and on the future price of gold, which we cannot foretell.

However, one should not think of the gold system, however established, as a system in which credit has no part. A gold standard is a system in which gold is the base of the credit pyramid of the world, but the pyramid is not itself built of blocks of bullion. On top of the gold base one has therefore to allow for changes in the quantity of credit; there is no question but that the credit pyramid will tend to expand faster than the gold base, but will expand only at a limited rate. The fact that the credit has to refer back to the gold base will constantly act to prevent an inflationary credit explosion.

The reason why credit grows faster than its money base is probably this. Since the development of modern banking began in the seventeenth century there has been a steady, though not uniform, increase in the complexity of the credit structure, and this increase in complexity has multiplied the effectiveness of credit. This complexification of banking will, except in circumstances of panic, continue, and may make good the shortfall of new mined gold against the desired growth of world business.

Nor should the gold system be regarded as one which is so purely automatic that it needs no management. Much of the benefit of the gold system came from the fact that central banks operated by its rules, and acted early as a result, before trends had become too strongly established. The Bretton Woods structure, with the International Monetary Fund and the central banks working together, is well suited to the organisation of a gold system. Indeed, so long as the dollar remained convertible, Bretton Woods was of course a gold and convertible currencies system, and from the American side was designed as such. The International Monetary Fund ought itself to remain the central bank for central banks, with its own stock of gold, and ought to be responsible for the favourable operation of the system.

The objection is often raised that there is not enough gold in the world, or that Britain does not have enough gold. The question of the amount of gold that is needed is partly a question of price, and partly of confidence. When the price of gold was frozen at $35 an ounce, over a period in which the dollar exchange system had financed a great increase in other prices, that certainly produced a situation in which there was too little gold to provide the ultimate reserve liquidity. Historically there has been no fixed ratio between world trade and the gold stock, but the free market has already moved gold to a level which is not obviously inappropriate.

An individual country does not need an enormous stock of gold, but it does need to have created a sufficiently strong belief that it can maintain its exchange rate. Confidence, not quantity of bullion, is the key condition to the successful operation of a gold standard. The need to maintain confidence rather than actual movement of bullion is why a gold standard does genuinely discipline the financial conduct of its members, and has its stabilising effect.

At the outbreak of the first world war the Bank of England, then still the centre of the gold standard exchange system, had a gold stock of a little over £40 million (£41,400,000 in the first quarter of 1914, the highest ever reported). At constant cost of living prices that would now be the equivalent of a stock of about £320 million, or at constant gold prices a stock of about £680 million. Of course, in 1914 Britain also had a gold currency which was a further, and psychologically highly effective, backing for the exchange rate.

One aim of a national gold policy is to create an identification in the public mind, nationally and internationally, between the national money and a particular quantity of gold. In the case of Britain this was first done by Edward III, who laid down in 1345 that a pound of gold of twenty-three carats, three and a half grains fineness, should be coined into 50 Florences, to be current at six shillings each. So that British currency under Edward III was fixed at £15 to the pound of gold, a rate subsequently changed. So long as it is believed that such a tie will be preserved, currency balances are as good as gold, and better in that they can be invested to produce income. Actual bullion only becomes important when it is thought that the nation will default on its gold commitment. Then you get the international equivalent of a run on the bank; to overcome that you need, and the I.M.F. would be, a gold lender of last resort.

The objective of a return to a gold standard is to return to a world currency of constant value. The objective would be completely fulfilled if there were total convertibility into and out of gold at fixed rates of all the major currencies, both in international settlement and eventually internally. The objective would be to include the Communist powers in this system, at any rate so far as international settlement is concerned. It is therefore no disadvantage that one of the Communist powers, the Soviet Union, is one of the world's two largest gold producers. If this makes the Soviet Union richer, so much the better. One must avoid the bullionist illusion that under a gold standard there is some special value to a gold mine; it is worth the gold it produces, just as an oil well is worth its oil production.

It is more of a disadvantage that the other main producer is South Africa, not because there is any objection to enriching South Africa, which may tend to accelerate the improvement in the condition of black South Africans. The objection is rather that the political and racial crisis which South Africa is liable to face might at some point interrupt gold production and therefore disturb the world currency system. That is a real risk to be guarded against through the organisation of world reserves, though it does not seem as grave a risk as the existing threat of inflation to the world monetary system and to the world's political stability.

In a gold system there is a tendency for trade balances to be stabilised; there is also much greater stability in the terms of trade. Great Britain has suffered an adverse movement of 25 per cent in her terms of trade in the past three years, resulting not surprisingly in a massive balance of payments deficit. Had the pound been tied to gold that movement would not have occurred.

Indeed, the great movement of oil prices reflected the oil-producing countries' reluctance to accept payment in currencies of constantly falling purchasing power. Neither the original inordinate expansion of the use of cheap Middle East oil, nor the inflation of currencies which made the oil producers determined to raise prices, nor the actual scale of the increases would have been likely to arise under a gold system. The gold ratios are surprisingly strong, and one saw that the rise in the oil price was accompanied by a comparable rise in the price of gold on the free market.

Obviously the oil countries will have, and should have, large surpluses, whatever system of pricing and currency is adopted. Yet the problem of investing these surpluses, as well as the problem of unstable movements in oil prices, would be easier to handle on a gold standard. Because gold holds its value, a prudent investor would hold, and historically has always held, longer dated, lower interest gold securities than paper securities. The flood of short-term Arab money, which is among other things further inflating the already inflated Euro-dollar market, is bound to be invested short term when the currencies on offer represent only short-term stores of value. What is needed is good money.

'Good money' has always been taken to mean money which is of lasting value, which performs the function of a store of value. This is the essential difference between gold and any paper money, that gold is indestructible, while paper money depends both on the continuance and on the self-restraint of the government of issue. Gold alone, or with silver, meets Locke's celebrated definition of money as 'some lasting thing that men might keep without spoiling, and that by mutual consent men would take in exchange for the truly useful, but perishable supports of life'. The crisis of oil prices and Arab money shows that paper does not meet Locke's definition – and what the consequences of failure to meet that definition must be. Only a 'lasting thing' can secure the 'mutual consent' which is essential both to the exchange of goods for money, and to the investment of the money received.

The adoption of a gold system would leave certain vital questions to be answered. What should be the price of gold relative to the key currencies? Probably a price closely related to the free market price at the time the system was introduced. Should the price of gold be changeable subsequently? Possibly the I.M.F. should have the power to devalue all currencies in terms of gold if a genuine shortage of liquidity threatened to produce a major world depression. Should currencies be fixed in terms of gold, and therefore also in terms of each other? Certainly yes. Should there be a trading margin? Probably not, though bullion trading would take place at a premium to pay the costs of the trade. Should there be provision for devaluations and revaluations? Recent experience has weakened the belief that devaluation or revaluation can be relied upon to correct imbalances of trade, but in extreme circumstances they may be inevitable. Can the Bretton Woods machinery, the I.M.F. with its powers, be used to supervise the gold system? Certainly yes.

These are important questions, but the central argument must be restated. Gold is the only permanent international currency. It is the most intelligible of all currencies. It is the only currency which provides a constant world money supply. It is the only currency with a good record as a long-term store of value. It is the only currency which naturally tends to stabilise prices, against both upward and downward movements, therefore acting against inflation and deflation. It is the only currency with a strong tendency to stabilise trade balances and the terms of trade. It is the only currency which naturally stabilises long-term interest rates at a low but positive level. It is a standard of value which allows a variable economic system to be co-ordinated.

Apart from the gold inflations, particularly those of Alexander the Great and Philip II, which happened for reasons most unlikely to recur, gold has a consistent record of actually securing price stability. Whenever and wherever gold currency has been used, long-term prices have been stable and short-term price movements have been moderated. The record of managed currencies is the opposite; no managed currency system, not linked to gold, has provided price stability, and most such systems have been grossly inflationary.

We are involved in a major world inflation, the worst in the world's history, which has now reached the stage when prices are still rising, but economic activity is being depressed. We have a choice between two systems, one of which has quite consistently prevented inflation, while the other, our present world monetary system, has consistently produced it. Neither system has consistently produced full employment, but rapid inflation has quite consistently produced heavy unemployment.

The freedom of action which is lost in restoring a gold system can now be seen to be illusory. It is in fact freedom to turn a stable system into an unstable one, a constant money supply into an inflated money supply, a self-equilibriating system into a self-destroying system, an objective system into a subjective one. The freedom of action which matters, that of choosing the form of society in which one wants to live, is actually strengthened by a gold standard; gold provides the price stability on which political societies can be made to survive.

Gold also imposes on man a respect for economic resources. The quantity of gold is finite, because gold is one of the mineral resources of the world. The quantity of oil, coal, copper or human labour is also finite. Gold belongs to the family of real economic resources whose exchange it is supposed to regulate.

Paper money is infinite; one can write down $100 or $100 million or $100,000,000 million on the same piece of paper; there is no shortage of noughts. If we measure finite resources in finite money we are less likely to indulge in the mania of extravagance that has marked the last fifteen years, that has squandered irreplaceable resources and polluted our planet. Sanity in society can be shown to depend on sanity in money; it appears that the same is true of sanity in the use of resources as well.

CHAPTER FIVE

CONQUERING THE MONSTER

Although the former debasement of the coins by public
authority, especially those in the reigns of King Henry the
Eighth, and King Edward the Sixth, might be projected for
the profit of the Crown; and the projectors might measure
that profit by the excessive quantities of allay that were
mixed with the silver or the gold: and although this was
enterprised by a Prince who could stretch his prerogative
very far upon his people; and was done in times when this
nation had very little commerce, inland or foreign, to be
injured or prejudiced thereby: yet experience presently
shewed that the projectors were mistaken, and that it was
absolutely necessary to have the base moneys reformed;
the doing whereof was begun by King Edward the Sixth
himself, carried on by King Philip and Queen Mary, and
happily finished (though not without great charge, vexation
and trouble, the only offspring of such designs) by Queen
Elizabeth who . . . in the third year of her reign, when
money was not plentiful, erected a distinct mint in the
Tower, to convert the base (not counterfeit money) into
sterling . . .

And here it may not be improper to note, that not long
after, the Queen in a public edict, told her people, that
she had conquered the Monster which had so long
devoured them; meaning the debasing of the standard.

*A Report containing an Essay for the Amendment
of the Silver Coins.* William Lowndes, 1695

The aim of a gold policy would be, in the very broadest terms,
to impose a system of order on currencies and prices, on the
world's money, and therefore on the world economy. We should
pay a price for this system of order, the price of loss of subjective control. Man would be accepting that an automatic

discipline is superior in its operation to any management he can devise for himself, that he cannot trust himself to operate a purely managed system in a way that will maintain stability. He may be brought to this conclusion by finding that his own system has collapsed; it will be difficult to bring him to it before the collapse occurs, but the attempt is essential.

The question that will be asked is whether a return to gold is feasible. Certainly it is feasible technically. There is nothing in the objection that there is not enough gold in the world, though any one nation may have an inadequate gold stock. The whole world cannot have too little gold, as the price can always be brought to a level at which the total stock is sufficient in value for the trade it has to finance.

There have indeed been numerous reconstructions of gold currencies, or restorations of gold standards, in the past. Gresham's reform of the Elizabethan currency is one example. Britain returned to the gold standard in 1821 and 1925, both times after inflations caused by war. After the Civil War the United States returned to the gold standard in 1879. The operation has been performed several times, usually with success.

There are two points to note about the technical problems of returning to full gold convertibility. The first is that it has to be phased; Peel's Act of 1819 which provided for convertibility in four years – in fact it was reached in two – is the best example. The second is that a choice has to be made between restoring some previous gold parity – which means forcing prices down to their pre-inflation level – or merely accepting the existing price level. In 1821, 1879 and 1925 the pre-war parity was chosen, and the process of forcing down prices caused industrial depression in Britain in the 1820s and the 1920s, and in the United States in the late 1870s.

Of course there would now be no question of trying to return to pre-war price levels, or to pre-war gold parities. We no more have to go back to the old mint price of £3.17s.10½d. an ounce for sterling, than we have to go back to the standard of £15 a pound of King Edward III. Equally, therefore, the problem of a gold-induced depression would not arise for that reason. The main criticism Keynes made of Churchill's return to gold in 1925, that it was unduly deflationary to return to the old price, would be removed. Some depression is likely to occur at the end of an inflation anyway, as the economy adjusts from a rising prices expectation to a stable price expectation. Churchill's return to the gold standard did not of course cause the slump five years later; that was the result of monetary policy mistakes in the United States, caused neither by Britain nor by the gold standard.

The success of restorations of gold convertibility depended not on the establishment of an enormous stock of gold, but on the creation of the belief that the price would not be changed. This confidence depended on a balanced budget, which observation showed had a strong tendency to produce a balance of the external account, and on a balance of trade, or at least a sufficiently consistent inflow of capital to offset trade deficits. This confidence was not shaken by temporary setbacks. In Professor Friedman's words, written of the 1879 resumption in the United States, 'the conditions for a successful resumption were not a razor's edge, but a broad band.'

What would be required therefore, technically, would be a decision to stabilise the currency and to return to gold, then a stabilisation programme, designed to balance the budget, limit growth of the money supply and correct the imbalance of overseas trade, and finally a return to convertibility at a price reflecting current price levels. The convertibility might, in the case of a country short of gold, have to be supported by loan agreements or actual loans to provide a standby credit sufficiently large to deal with any possible speculative attack.

The pre-resumption stabilisation programme for Britain might be very similar to the policies of Mr Jenkins' chancellorship, from 1967 to 1970, which did in fact create an overall balance of the budget, stabilised the money supply, and produced a trade surplus of £1,000 million. Present oil prices would probably make such a surplus unattainable for Britain before the late 1970s. Unemployment would inevitably rise, as it did after Mr Jenkins' period, but from now on inflation itself is a far greater threat to employment than any stabilisation programme.

The essential quality of any good monetary stabilisation programme is that it should be gradual. Sudden changes in the money supply always destabilise, and exaggerated and rapid reductions in an inflationary trend can lead ´ ˋ panic and to avoidable unemployment. A slow and gentle return to monetary stability over a period of years is the right way to bring inflation under control; over-sudden contractions are often prematurely reversed and undo their own work.

It must be emphasised that the operation of the gold standard has not, historically, resulted in particularly high long-term unemployment. It is these sharp reductions in the real money supply, as economists from Ricardo to Professor Friedman have consistently shown, that lead to rises in unemployment. The whole objective of a gold standard policy is to stabilise the money supply, and avoid both sharp reductions and sharp increases.

It is notable that Peel's Act, perhaps the best of these resumption schemes, in which he was assisted by Ricardo, was itself attacked on still familiar grounds. He had to defend the case for gold, saying that he believed 'the old, the vulgar doctrine, as some have called it, that the true standard of value consisted of a definite quantity of gold bullion'. The gold standard was already old and vulgar in 1819, at the start of its century of greatest service. Its very simplicity disgusts some minds; any fool can say what a gold pound is worth; it is worth its weight in gold; it takes a wise man to recognise that he does not know what a paper pound is worth.

There is therefore no great technical difficulty in drafting or enacting a stabilisation programme or a resumption of gold payments. There may be difficulties for particular countries in creating the confidence which would make the conditions for successful resumption, 'a broad band'. In particular there is an enormous mass of floating money – both the oil money in Arab and other hands and more than $150 billion in Euro-currencies – which would have to be stabilised. The oil countries would benefit very substantially from the positive rate of interest available from gold standard countries, and they would need to be brought in as partners in the stabilisation of world currencies and the resumption of gold convertibility. The Euro-currency markets must, gold or no gold, be brought under control; their present capacity to create vast new liquid credits makes them a dangerous force of instability.

Above all, a successful gold system needs strength; it needs the absolute confidence in the maintenance of the basic gold parities, a confidence that can best be achieved by a few strong partners. It is a system which the weak may be forced to adopt because of the collapse of their currencies, but the strong should be the cornerstones.

The obvious centres of strength are the United States, the Soviet Union, the European Economic Community and the oil countries. The United States, with Dr Burns' policies at the Federal Reserve Board and President Ford's appeal to Congress for Budget cuts, is already trying to pursue those balanced financial policies which would make a return to gold convertibility possible. Such policies would indeed be greatly strengthened by the expectation of a return to gold before the possible end of the Ford Presidency, that is by the end of the decade. The Soviet Union is already a very large gold producer, and the rouble is supported as a hard currency by the Russian gold reserves.

A single gold currency is now perhaps the most likely way in which a single European currency could be achieved. It would have ample gold backing; the modest gold reserves of Britain are matched by large German, French and Italian reserves. There is every prospect that the E.E.C. as a single trading group will have a favourable long-term balance of trade, certainly when the North Sea oil flow reaches its projected level.

For Britain the advantages would be great. We should be able to move to gold convertibility more rapidly than we could on our own, before the benefits of the North Sea had fully accrued. The gold parity would be secured against ample total reserves and trading power. The price for Britain would involve following balanced Budget policies which we shall be obliged to follow anyway, if the pound is not to collapse under the weight of our present deficits. It is true that if we inflated wages faster than other European countries we would suffer in exports and employment; any system of ending inflation would, however, impose exactly this penalty on wage inflation, a European currency no more than any other system, and with a better prospect of assistance in overcoming our problems. For the whole European Community the advantage would be the restoration of price stability, and the prospect of long-term price stability. For every nation in the European Community the greatest possible dangers would be averted, and new opportunities of stable economic development would be open.

This new gold standard, based on the three great economic powers of the United States, the Soviet Union and Europe, and with the partnership of the oil powers, could be administered by the International Monetary Fund, at least so far as the non-Communist world is concerned. With four such strong partners a gold lender of last resort would have a smaller part to play, but would still be desirable, particularly for the largest of what would be the secondary powers in the system, such as Japan.

What are the chances of such reforms being adopted? That must depend on events. Great political decisions are influenced by argument, but determined by happenings; in this case we have the strength of gold, the weakness of paper and the acceleration of world inflation all acting in the same direction. Argument and discussion can ease the passage to gold resumption, but gold will be restored, if at all, because gold is strong and paper is weak – not because the arguments are accepted, but because they are true.

The present support for gold varies from country to country. The most important country is the United States; there the signs are favourable, but only in a preliminary way. Certainly the question of gold is seriously discussed. Monetarist economics lead the mind naturally to the question of gold, just as Keynesian economics lead the mind naturally away from it. The decision by Congress to allow private purchases of gold is very significant as an indication of changing attitudes. In private conversations in Washington this year I found that the gold question was being taken increasingly seriously, though most people were not yet ready to accept the conclusions of the gold argument.

In Continental Europe gold is better understood because European countries have suffered 'wipe-out' inflations, and have found the truth that gold retains its purchasing power in circumstances in which the purchasing power of paper is destroyed. For instance, the reason that French families try to keep a private gold reserve is not that they are stupid peasants, as some economists suppose. It is that France was invaded three times in a century, and French families discovered that you could, quite literally, trust your life to gold and not to paper.

Gold would buy petrol to get you to the coast; paper would not. If you had to survive an occupation, gold would buy you food; paper would not. France has also been influenced by the work of M. Rueff, an internationalist French economist who has performed as great a service by his advocacy of gold as M. Monnet by his advocacy of Europe. Germany is not committed to any gold sympathies, but is totally committed to the attack on inflation, if possible by European agreement.

It is in Britain that the idea of gold is unfamiliar. Britain was naturally at the centre of the Keynesian economic revolution, but has not been equally the centre of the recent development of economic theory. A generation of economists has been brought up to believe that there was no case in the 1920s for the Bank of England, and that Keynes was not only brilliant, but obviously right. It must also be admitted that Keynes' least attractive attitude, his intellectual arrogance, has influenced the personalities of some of his successors. Since the war British economic policy and policy discussion have failed to produce a coherent response to the growing inflationary threat.

It is not, however, the theoretical or the technical questions which people are most concerned about. The argument that has to be met is whether there has been such a radical change in social circumstances and in economic power that a system which was feasible in the nineteenth century is not feasible now. Ought we to accept the fact that the development of the trade unions condemns us to permanent inflation, and that a gold standard, even if it were ideal as a way of securing price stability, is unattainable?

There is one preliminary and powerful answer to that. Price instability is not itself stable. The belief that it is possible to have controlled inflation in a managed currency system, and keep inflation down to a tolerable and constant rate, is not supported by experience. The choice for the late twentieth century is not one between stable prices and stable trade union-induced inflation, but one between stable prices and accelerating inflation. It is not a choice between two systems, either of which can be made to work, but between two systems, of which one works and the other explodes.

It may be true that at this stage the forces of inflation – at least in Britain and some other countries – are too strong to allow a gold standard to work; that is the pessimistic view, but it cannot be excluded. If this is true, we face catastrophe, but catastrophe in which trade union power itself will be involved. Certainly trade union power makes it much more difficult to stop inflation now, but at this stage inflation begins to eat into the power of the trade unions, and particularly into the loyalty of their members.

One has to follow through what will happen if catastrophe does occur. The logical end of inflation is that money, like the assignats, or the German mark, loses its purchasing power totally. It becomes quite worthless; at one point the mark was worth more as waste paper than as currency, at least in most denominations. That leads logically to a situation of zero value for money, zero real money supply, and something close to zero business activity and employment. And one can see that there is another zero to be added, zero trade union bargaining power. In such conditions the trade unions may survive, even very powerfully, as political associations, but they are left with no economic power and no ability to protect their members. In terminal inflation there is no valued money and no work; not a favourable situation for strike action.

This is more than a theoretical point. We have seen that union power tends to increase in the early stages of inflation. Even by the present stage of the world inflation, the effect on union power has become selective, with the power of the strong unions rising, while that of weak unions is actually falling. If the end of inflation reduces union power to zero – as it certainly did in Germany – there must come a point at which even the strongest unions can see that their power is actually declining. In Britain we might reach that point if, say, there were a further doubling of the rate of inflation, and at an even earlier point the different consequences for different unions would be likely to strain the unity of the trade union movement.

There is also a more positive case to consider. Just as much as anyone else, trade unionists and social democrats are looking for a way out of inflation, and indeed desperately need to find one. It is already probable in Britain that the T.U.C. policy – consumer subsidies, economic expansion and voluntary wage restraint – is not going to provide the answer. Yet the record of European social democratic governments is not outstandingly inflationary, as compared with governments of the centre or right. In Germany Herr Schmidt has an unquestioned record for his opposition to inflation. In Britain the two great anti-inflationary Chancellors of the Exchequer have been Sir Stafford Cripps and Mr Jenkins, both Labour. Whatever their intellectual reluctance, there is no reason why social democrats and trade unionists should not look at the case for gold on its merits; of course the far left will not do so; politically they can hope for advantage from the ruin that inflation brings.

Social democracy is concerned with social justice and welfare, and believes that state power must be used to pursue them both. Moderate trade unionism is concerned with improving the real earnings and working conditions of trade unionists, and securing their jobs. None of these objectives is compatible with inflation; all are compatible with the gold standard as it worked historically.

Among the social democratic parties of Western Europe the monetarist argument is already well understood, though gold is still rejected, mainly because of the historic association between gold resumptions and depression, partly because, in less logical terms, gold is thought of as inhuman and archaic. Gold is inhuman in the sense that it prevents humans from indulging in the pleasures of inflation, and it is archaic in the sense that it has held value for 2,500 years since it was first coined by King Croesus of Lydia.

Yet if the parties of the left understand that those who believe in gold – and this is particularly true of M. Rueff – do so because they regard it as a discipline calculated to promote prosperity and stability, they may view the emergence of gold under the pressure of events with less hostility. The argument for gold is an argument against the injustices of inflation and for a restoration of real values, including the stabilising and improvement of the real value of wages. It would be a pity if the advocacy of restoration of gold became isolated as a right-wing privilege. Inevitably a gold standard introduced with general support would have a better prospect than one introduced by a right-wing government against socialist opposition. The need to make welfare systems work, to maintain or improve the value of pensions, to stabilise the real pay of civil servants and trade unionists and to reduce interest rates, could all move social democratic governments towards a gold standard. Above all, however, it is important that the left should realise that gold, as opposed to tight money, is equilibriating and not depressant to prices and employment.

The obstacles to reform are formidable, but they are not necessarily insuperable. The question remains, whether reform will come in time. Can we contain and then terminate the process of inflation, or are we going to be destroyed by inflation before we decide to restore a stable system?

This is the question of the survival of democracy. Technically there is nothing which has to be done which a democracy cannot do. The British Government could propose, and the British Parliament could enact, a suitable modernisation of Peel's Act, introducing phased convertibility at a fixed exchange rate, perhaps before 1980. The European Governments could discuss proposals to adhere to a European currency unit in gold, again perhaps by 1980, and if they were agreed could introduce them. The United States Congress could enact and the President could approve legislation to end the second greenback inflation in the way they ended the first, by a second Resumption Act.

There is at least nothing in this which requires resort to non-democratic means. No colonels, no tanks, no prison camps, no secret policemen are needed to enact or carry through balanced budgets, currency reforms or gold convertibility. Yet there is a more fundamental question than that. Can we obtain the consent of democracies to the ending of inflation? Will democracies consent to their own survival?

This again is not a new question. The last time it was posed in the extreme form was in the years before 1939. Democracy then had to be persuaded to agree to rearmament and to a firm policy in dealing with aggression. Neither American or British nor French democracy responded adequately to that call. The United States held an ample margin of safety; they had the Atlantic. In Britain we had a sufficient margin of safety; we had the Channel. France did not, and for five years French democracy was eclipsed. But all countries were inadequate in rearmament, the more remote the slower, and all were inadequate in diplomacy – Britain and France signed the Munich Treaty; the United States was isolationist.

The condition of survival in those years was that democracies had to be persuaded to face immediate sacrifices for long-term security. That is exactly the point at which democracy is weakest. There is always somebody to argue that the sacrifices are not necessary (a British Labour Party poster in the 1935 election had the slogan, 'A Vote for Rearmament is a Vote for War'.) The electorate, sometimes rightly, judges by immediate appearances and regards long-term consequences as hypothetical. Electorates tend to value the immediate too highly against the long term.

Any policy for ending inflation will cause some measure of immediate dislocation, some distress, some further bankruptcies, some rise in unemployment. Gold will, on the argument of this essay, actually cause the least dislocation, but it will cause some. Democracy has to be asked to accept this immediate sacrifice, and in the case of gold, democracy has to be asked to accept arguments which, although familiar to past generations and to other countries, are not familiar to the present generation in Britain or the United States.

Gold has no politics; it has been the servant of every type of potentate and every type of constitution. Yet there is a temper of political mind which ought to feel a natural sympathy with it. A gold system works through the money supply and does not require an elaborate system of controls; it should appeal to the political liberal. Gold is international; it is the world's money supply; it is natural for a man who believes in gold to be internationalist rather than nationalist in outlook. Gold is stable; it not only represents order, it imposes order by a quasi-automatic mechanism; it should appeal to the institutional conservative. Gold is just; it deals equally between one man and another, between past, present and future; it does not take from the weak to give to the strong; it should appeal to the seeker of social justice, to the social democrat.

Yet above everything else gold is ordinate. There is a given total quantity which has been found and refined over several thousand years of work. It can only be added to little by little. It can therefore act as the unchanging discipline of the economic system.

The reason that democracy works is that it too is an ordinate system. Even more than by the choice which is inherent in democracy, the system works because of the discipline that democracy imposes on government. Under a gold standard, economic activity is shaped both by what gold does – flowing in or flowing out – and by what gold might do – the threat of an outflow; in the same way, in democracy the acts of government are shaped not only by what the electorate does – electing or not electing – but also by what the electorate might do – the possible withdrawal of support. The pressing and continuous discipline of an absolute – the world's stock of money in the one case and the public will in the other – does not only decide matters at moments of crisis to the system. It shapes matters from day to day, so that the extreme crises may not occur.

Democracy depends for its survival on the defence of its own disciplines. The first of these is the constitution; an unconstitutional democracy is a contradiction in terms. The constitution is the matrix from which the operation of the democracy is the impression; the constitution is also the form which the citizen who wants to defend democracy sees that he must defend. Indeed democracy is not merely a general abstract system in which all citizens have the right to vote; where it is strongest it is most clearly particular and concrete, not 'all citizens have the right to vote' but all citizens over the age of eighteen on the due date, excepting peers and some others, have the right to vote in the places where they are registered on the electoral roll. It is in the definition of detail that the security of democracy lies, and a democracy which does not place value on its own constitution will not survive.

In Britain democracy grew out of the constitution. In the beginning there was the sovereignty of the king (and Shapespeare's Richard II shows how vital the legitimacy of the Crown still seemed to an Elizabethan). Then came the sovereignty of the king under the law; then the sovereignty of the king in Parliament, both central issues of the Civil War. Then later comes the sovereignty of a democratically elected Parliament, with full adult suffrage only in this century. In the United States the constitution itself is democratic, and the state was founded on a democratic basis, though less fully democratic than it is today. In both countries democracy could not survive without the constitution, which not only preserves it and gives it validity, but gives it functional shape and effectiveness.

More broadly, democracy depends not only on constitution

but also on law. Unless people respect the law which governs their relations with each other and with the state, then no constitution, however sound, can prevent the nation slipping into anarchy. Democracy indeed depends not only on the will of the majority, but on almost universal consent. We have seen in recent history how very small groups, who put themselves into the position of outlaws, can disrupt society.

Democracy also requires loyalty. In war democracy survives only because there are young men brave enough and loyal enough to die for their country. Even in peacetime some young men have to be willing to accept that risk for democracy to survive. The lives of free nations are founded on the deaths of brave men.

It is for this reason that President de Gaulle's concept of *L'Europe des Patries* is psychologically so sound. The nations need Europe, need the collective idea, if they are to act effectively in the world; Europe is potentially stronger than its parts, because the most extreme weaknesses of each individual nation are not found universally through the community. Yet it is the nations which are the focus of loyalty, and for generations no Europe will be strong which does not express rather than try to replace this patriotism.

Democracy also needs another quality; one that used rather disagreeably to be called national pride; it is probably better termed self-esteem. Nations should think well of themselves. In the twentieth century they need to feel that their social arrangements are fair and their economic achievements valuable. A democratic nation which thinks too little of itself is likely to think too little of democracy.

These then are the conditions of democracy: constitution, law, loyalty and a certain self-esteem. Yet can one deny that democracy also needs economic stability both as a discipline and as a foundation? Keynes wrote that it was doubtful whether individual capitalism could survive without a standard of value – he meant without gold – and proceeded to destroy that standard of value. Yet if that is true of individual capitalism, is it not equally true of social democracy? Is it not true of democracy as such?

Let us put the argument in its simplest terms. All human institutions require a limit, if they are not to become inordinate;

they need an objective governor. For money gold is such a governor; no gold standard has produced inordinate inflation, most have produced price stability; no pure paper system has produced price stability, many have produced inordinate inflation; democracy is an ordinate system of human government; it has often been destroyed by inflation, sometimes by deflation, never by price stability. If we successfully restore a gold standard we shall destroy inflation, probably in the only way it can be destroyed. We shall restore price stability and remove a serious threat to democracy.

This comes back to the starting point. Inordinacy always ends in ruin, and inordinacy can only be controlled by systems that are objective and external, rather than by purely subjective restraints. The reigning error of the twentieth century is just this, the rejection of the idea of external discipline. The damage that Dr Spock did was that he destroyed confidence in discipline for children; the damage that Freud did was that he destroyed belief in the necessity of discipline in sexual conduct; the damage of the explosion of science was that it destroyed discipline in man's dealings with nature. Keynes made an equally profound attack on the idea of discipline in money.

All these things were done with good intentions; they rejected discipline because they wanted a world in which no children cried, no one was sexually distressed, no one was deprived of any natural resource, a world in which the sun would shine every day of the week. Keynes in particular wanted to destroy the limits on economic progress, and particularly the limit of unemployment.

Who can quarrel with such kindly intentions? Who would not like an earthly paradise, or sympathise with those who worked to bring one about? Yet the enterprise of removing suffering from the world is a dangerous one. Suppose that the suffering turns out to be necessary to avert greater sufferings, suppose that suffering is necessary to successful adjustment to the real conditions of life, how is one to deal with that?

The sanction of any economic discipline, of the discipline which adjusts economic affairs to changing reality is the reduction of economic activity. This means that there will be less profit, or loss, for business, less revenue for the state, less employment and therefore a rise in unemployment. This is true of all types of demand management, not only of gold or monetary policy. The alternative to this discipline is either to have no discipline at all, which is sure to lead to inflation, or to substitute non-economic disciplines, controls by the state, and the use of compulsion.

Any of these disciplines cause hardship and suffering. In Communist systems the ultimate form of the suffering is imprisonment, forced non-economic labour, or even death. In free market systems it is unemployment. Yet the more stable the control system is, the less discipline will be incurred. A stable gold system, once established, should revert to full employment, provided wages are not raised above the level that can be earned in each job. Unemployment can also be alleviated by unemployment benefit.

When the world inflation is brought to an end or collapses, there is likely to be widespread unemployment for some time, caused not by the new sound money, but by the logic of inflation, by the collapse of the purchasing power of the old bad money. It is the task of economic management to minimise this unemployment; it is, however, wrong to pretend that economic systems can be controlled without any disciplines at all, for that is to say that they can be controlled without control.

The advantage of an automatic, or quasi-automatic system, such as gold, is that it acts through constant minor adjustments, successive minor acts of discipline, rather than allowing the system to build up pressure to the point of explosion. It does not aim at constant flat-out operation of the economy, but at stable and sustained operation, with employment more secure than it is in an inflationary economy, but with the level of employment subject to the use of economic disciplines. It is wrong to deny that a gold system, or any demand-influencing system, uses unemployment as a part of its continuous discipline; equally it is wrong to imagine that gold or monetary discipline is likely to lead to the slump levels of unemployment which normally follow inflation.

To be cruel to be kind is usually an act of hypocrisy, but it has perhaps done less harm than the twentieth-century vice of being too kind to be kind. The most fundamental relationships of human life have been re-engineered in order to prevent sufferings which turned out to represent the unavoidable limitations of human existence. This was wrong not because of the kindness but because of the inordinate attitudes which underlay the genuine desire to help.

The Keynesian revolution was one of these revolutions of kindness; he took the fine old Rolls-Royce of nineteenth-century economics and rebuilt it with every modern sophistication, but without the brakes. He associated brakes with suffering. We have reason now to associate not having brakes with suffering.

Yet even if one is convinced of the need for an economic standard of value, for an economic discipline strong enough to end inflation and therefore strong enough to save democracy, there is a further point to guard against. The discipline which saves democracy will not be a discipline of fear, it will be a discipline of love; it must not be a discipline that repels people, but one that draws people towards it.

That is the point of Maimonides' statement about the Torah; he assumes that to many the ordinances will seem burdensome, and that it is therefore necessary to show the purpose behind the discipline. The same principle applies to all disciplines, divine and human; they must be known to have meaning and they must be shown to be for the genuine good of those who undertake them. The discipline of gold is only justified if it is, or can be made to be, a discipline not only of suffering – though the limitation of all discipline implies the possibility of suffering – but of stability leading to prosperity.

The prize is very great. Good money means stable prices, not for a month but for a century at a time; stable prices guard against the extremes of both boom and slump. Good money restores reality to the payment for work and to saving. It permits not only the businessman but every citizen to plan his economic life ahead, and fulfil his own plans. It gives a real target not only to great ambitions but also to humble ones. It provides a solid platform for democratic government. It brings inflation to an end. Above all, good money would restore the sanity, the limited and proportionate character, of economic life. It would rid the world not only of inflation, but of the economic hubris which is worse even than inflation itself.

CRISIS OF PAPER CURRENCIES

The final blow to confidence came on September 15 (1931) when the men of the Atlantic Fleet at Invergordon refused duty in protest against the cuts in lower-deck pay, some of which exceeded 10 per cent. The Board of Admiralty promised a revision, and the more extreme cuts were in fact reduced.

It was too late. The foreign holders of sterling were in wild alarm. On 19 September the Bank of England reported that the foreign credits were exhausted. Two days later an Act suspending the gold standard was rushed through Parliament. The value of the pound fell by more than a quarter on the foreign exchange. Otherwise nothing happened. Englishmen had been using paper money for 17 years. They had forgotten the gold sovereign, and their paper pound seemed to them just as valuable as it had been before. This anticlimax took everyone by surprise. Passfield spoke for all his late colleagues (the previous Labour Government) when he complained 'Nobody told us we could do this'.

A. J. P. Taylor, English History 1914–1945

Could we be in this postion once again, but in reverse? Is it possible that just as the chronic deflationary disease of the early 1930s was relieved by abandoning the gold standard – a gold standard fixed at too high a rate for the pound – so the chronic inflationary disease of the mid-1970s could be relieved by returning to the gold standard – but to a gold standard fixed at a realistic and competitive rate for the pound?

Certainly this is one of those things which nobody tells us we could do. It is an option almost unmentioned among the world's leading academic economists, our leading central bankers, or our Treasury officials. There is discussion of almost every kind of floating or fixed paper system – nothing is so bizarre it has not been suggested – but there is little or no discuusion outside France of the implications for gold of the progressive failure of all the paper systems.

A gold standard simply involves the free convertibility of a currency or currencies into gold at a fixed price. No price is eternal, but once the price is fixed it becomes the chief aim of economic policy to maintain it, not as a fetish but as the axle of the economy. Such an arrangement is to some extent self-regulating; a strong currency attracts gold deposits which expand the credit base and increase economic activity, including imports, while a weak currency loses gold, with a consequent reduction in the credit base, a rise in interest rates, and a fall in activity and imports. Of course to return to a gold standard, or to the more flexible gold exchange system, there have to be adequate reserves, a maintainable price for the currency and at least international co-operation.

In managed paper currencies there is a natural conflict between short-term and long-term expediency. Long-term expediency puts a high premium on the maintenance of the value of the currency; in order to maintain its value it should be managed so as to be relatively scarce. Short-term expediency requires that the economy should be in a state of boom or near boom, and that interest rates should be as low as possible. At any given moment short-term advantage requires that the money supply should be increased, though the longer-term effect of increasing the money supply is to raise prices, and, as we now see, in the longer run expanding the money supply leads through higher prices to higher and not lower interest rates.

In a democracy, with elections occurring frequently and regularly, there is always a powerful pressure for short-term expediency. Economic management is subordinated to the need to win elections; some critics consider it is being so subordinated now; it certainly was so subordinated in every election since 1955, with the exception only of 1970, which was lost by the government of the day. Perhaps 1974 is a special case; the money supply was increased irresponsibly earlier in the Parliament but the election, also lost, was fought by the government on the issue of inflation.

Before 1931 it was forecast by the advocates of the gold

standard that democracies with managed currencies would be persistently and destructively inflationary. For instance, in January 1925, Montagu Norman, then Governor of the Bank of England, told Benjamin Strong, the Governor of the Federal Reserve Bank of New York, that a continuation of floating exchange rates would be 'an incentive to governments at times to undertake various types of paper money expedients and inflation . . . after some attempt at some other mechanism for the regulation of credit and prices, some kind of monetary crisis would finally result in ultimately restoring gold to its former position, but only after a period of hardship and suffering, and possibly some social and political disorder'.

Why, one may ask, has it taken fifty years for this forecast to look as though it were coming true? The chief reason is that a gold-dollar standard covered most of those fifty years, if imperfectly. Within a couple of years after 1931, which was a period of acute world deflation, there was informal and then formal stabilisation between the pound and the dollar.

After Bretton Woods and until 1971, when the dollar was declared formally inconvertible in order to halt the drain on the u.s. gold reserves, Britain and the other members of the International Monetary Fund were on a gold exchange standard; their currencies had a fixed relationship with the dollar and the dollar had a fixed and convertible relationship and convertible relationship with gold. Thus Britain, apart from a short period after 1931, remained on the gold standard, though with devaluation at lengthy intervals, and only at second hand through the dollar. Since 1968 there has been a free market in gold and the dollar's convertibility into gold has been theoretical rather than real.

The period of the dollar exchange standard also benefited from the continuation of the confidence in currencies that the astonishing success of the sterling gold standard had established in the nineteenth century. Between the Napoleonic war and the first world war, with full gold convertibility for much the greater part of that time, the purchasing power of the pound was virtually constant or gradually strengthening. A loaf cost 10.2d in 1820; 5.1d in 1895; long-term interest rates were $4\frac{1}{2}$ per cent in 1820; 3 per cent in 1910; yet there had been a rise in real standards of living, the index of money wages came to 110 in 1820; 181 in 1906. After a century of stable money, healthy economic habits had been formed which even now have not wholly been destroyed, habits of thrift, habits of investment in government securities, the acceptance of long-term money contracts of all kinds. If you believe money to be a store of value, it will for a long time continue to be one, even if deteriorating in its reliability.

Since the dollar ceased to be convertible into gold, a period still only of $2\frac{1}{2}$ years, the world itself has been taken off the gold standard. The results are already apparent and they are disastrous. World inflation, which is a disease of world currencies, has immensely accelerated in all the non-Communist countries. The hardship and suffering have already occurred, and the social and political disorder may not be far behind.

At the same time there has been no inflation at all in prices expressed in terms of gold, if one treats gold as the only non-managed world currency. When convertibility was suspended, the free market price of gold was $43; it has risen to over $175. In other words the gold value of the dollar has fallen by 75 per cent. If one compares that with the movements of commodity prices, or even property prices, one finds that there has been a considerable degree of stability. Your London house may be worth twice what it was three years ago; so may an acre of land in Wiltshire. Yet the fine town house or the acre of good farm land are still worth much the same number of ounces of gold as they were in 1960. So indeed would be the gallon of petrol you put in your car. At a time of extreme inflation of currencies, gold has quietly provided what money is for, a stable medium of exchange and standard of value. Gold works, but paper, unless based ultimately on gold, does not. Gold is real money and paper is pretend money.

This must, after all, be true. What determines the money value of owning a painting? – that it is unique. If a Rembrandt could be infinitely reduplicated, and perfectly reduplicated – so that it was the same thing – it would have a value only equal to the cost of the reduplication process. All currency depends for its value on the belief that it will not be reduplicated. That means that a pound depends on one's belief that Mr Wilson will not add to the number of pounds in circulation; a franc depends on the self-restraint of President X; a dollar depends on the relationship between President Nixon and the Federal Reserve.

Paper money is only as good as the men who control it, and they are under consistent pressures to print more of it. Gold exists in limited and finite quantity, and is added to by new production in limited and reasonably predictable quantity. The value of paper money is therefore precisely the value of a politician's promise, as high or as low as you put that; the value of gold, or of a contractual right to gold, is protected by the inability of politicians to manufacture it.

Of course, in any system the base has a superstructure of credit which multiplies its effective purchasing power. A gold base, however, because it is finite, imposes its own discipline on the structure of credit which can be built on it. A paper base is capable of unlimited management, and therefore the disciplines are much weaker. Inflation is limited only when men believe there is no more money to be had; with paper money that belief is virtually impossible to create, and can never really be justified.

It is argued against the restoration of gold to a central position in the world exchange system that it would greatly benefit, or might greatly benefit, the two largest gold producers, South Africa and the Soviet Union. This not a strong argument. The free market in gold is already providing much higher prices. There is no reason to think that greater wealth will make either South Africa or the Soviet Union less tolerable to us. Prosperity might equally well strengthen the peaceable elements in the Soviet Union and the progress of the black people of South Africa. In any case it is absurd to compare the small benefit to the Soviet Union of a higher gold price with the great benefit to world communism of the total inflationary collapse of our paper currencies.

What would be the benefit to Britain of a return to the gold standard? Ideally it should involve full internal and external convertibility into gold. Some of our problems would simply disappear. For instance, mortgage rates payable in gold, or gold backed paper, on a gold loan, would fall quite rapidly, perhaps to 5 per cent or below. House prices would be stabilised, and might even tend to decline somewhat. If new lettings in terms of a gold rent occurred, much property would be expected to come on the letting market. Gold wages would be paid, but would have to be earned in gold. Of course, it would not be customary to pay in sovereigns, but the promise to pay a pound would represent a genuine contractual commitment to pay a given amount of gold on demand. If, say, gold were fixed at £100 a fine ounce, and the currency were reorganised so that £1 new replaced £10 of existing currency, £1 new would have a gold equivalent of one-tenth ounce.

The whole problem of accounting for inflation would disappear, as depreciation would be charged in gold expenditure. For industry the combination of lower interest rates, stable prices and an end to taxation on inflationary profits would be favourable. Borrowing on world markets might probably be much less necessary, but so long as the gold clause was trusted, it would be easy to borrow at low rates of interest. Currency speculation would be discouraged but not abolished. The discipline necessary for a healthy balance of payments would be imposed by the need to protect the currency.

The broader problems of speculation, and the diversion of resources to speculation, would also be greatly reduced. Of course prices would still change; a good harvest would cheapen wheat, a strike in Chile would raise the price of copper. But gold-determined prices would not move automatically. The historic benefit of gold is that it sets a standard by which prices can be stabilised.

Obviously a gold-based currency provides a foundation for the operation of classical free market economic theory. The weakness of Mr Powell's revival of classical economics is that he prefers to base it on floating currencies; floating currencies may sometimes be unavoidable but always tend to be inflationary. A return to gold would not, however, automatically solve the problem of wage demands by monopoly trade unions, nor even obviate the need for wage restraint, though gold wages would have a stable value and that would tend to moderate wage pressures. If monopoly unions priced their labour out of the world market, they would put their members out of work.

What, then, is the price? Ut is no less than this. Britain would have to conduct her economic affairs with the overriding object of maintaining the value of her currency; that is to say of staying on the gold standard. We should have to give absolute priority to earning our living in the world and to living within what we could earn. We should be tearing up the full employ-ment commitment of the 1944 White Paper, a great political and economic revolution.

This would until very recently have seemed a high price to pay; now it is no great price at all. There is little or no prospect of maintaining full employment with the present inflation, in Britain or in the world. The full employment standard became a commitment to inflation, but the inflation has now accelerated past the point at which it is compatible with full employment.

Should we do this, if necessary, alone and now? If the world would co-operate we ought to, but we are not likely to do so. What is now most likely to happen is that world inflation will continue, without serious check, until it reaches the point at which it can no longer be supported as a world phenomenon. In British politcal terms one can only expect the party that wins the next election to be quite ineffective in its policies to-wards inflation, and to be involved in ruinous inflationary con-sequences. If we fail to prevent further increase in the geometric progression in world inflation, the party held responsible in each country could well be out of office for 10 to 20 years, as occurred after 1931. The first 1974 election showed that the floating pound and a statutory incomes policy simply does not have enough public support to protect Britain against inflation.

The decisive crisis will in any case not be in Britain, now merely a weak province of a decaying currency system, but at the centre in the United States. It may not come until the next cycle of recession and boom. Until the centre fails, the extre-mities may well be supported, but when the centre fails, the extremities will fail also. Politicians seldom move ahead of events, and the attempt to do so can be broken for want of public support, but events will in due course destroy the floating paper system. The refusal of the oil-producing countries to accept depreciating paper currencies at the old rate for their oil shows what happens to a currency system which cannot command confidence. After only two and a half years, the pure paper system has already reached the point at which world inflation is averaging some 15 per cent in the non-communist countries. When the paper system collapses, the survivors will dig in the rubble and they will find gold.